P9-DWX-547

# Index

* Rhode Island did not send any delegates to the Constitutional Convention.

Cover painting (1817) by John Trumbull (1756–1843)
The source for this book: http://archives.gov

*Note: The following text is a transcription of the Stone Engraving of the parchment Declaration of Independence (the document on display in the Rotunda at the National Archives Museum.) The spelling and punctuation reflects the original.*

## IN CONGRESS, JULY 4, 1776

The unanimous Declaration of the thirteen united States of America

When in the Course of human events it becomes necessary for one people to dissolve the political bands which have connected them with another and to assume among the powers of the earth, the separate and equal station to which the Laws of Nature and of Nature's God entitle them, a decent respect to the opinions of mankind requires that they should declare the causes which impel them to the separation.

We hold these truths to be self-evident, that all men are created equal, that they are endowed by their Creator with certain unalienable Rights, that among these are Life, Liberty and the pursuit of Happiness. - That to secure these rights, Governments are instituted among Men, deriving their just powers from the consent of the governed, - That whenever any Form of Government becomes destructive of these ends, it is the Right of the People to alter or to abolish it, and to institute new Government, laying its foundation on such principles and organizing its powers in such form, as to them shall seem most likely to effect their Safety and Happiness. Prudence, indeed, will dictate that Governments long established should not be changed for light and transient causes; and accordingly all experience hath shewn that mankind are more disposed to suffer, while evils are sufferable than to right themselves by abolishing the forms to which they are accustomed. But when a long train of abuses and usurpations, pursuing invariably the same Object evinces a design to reduce them under absolute Despotism, it is their right, it is their duty, to throw off such Government, and to provide new Guards for their future security. - Such has been the patient sufferance of these Colonies; and such is now the necessity which constrains them to alter their former Systems of Government. The history of the present King of Great Britain is a history of repeated injuries and usurpations, all having in direct object the establishment of an absolute Tyranny over these States. To prove this, let Facts be submitted to a candid world.

He has refused his Assent to Laws, the most wholesome and necessary for the public good.

He has forbidden his Governors to pass Laws of immediate and pressing importance, unless suspended in their operation till his Assent should be obtained; and when so suspended, he has utterly neglected to attend to them.

He has refused to pass other Laws for the accommodation of large districts of people, unless those people would relinquish the right of Representation in the Legislature, a right inestimable to them and formidable to tyrants only.

He has called together legislative bodies at places unusual, uncomfortable, and distant from the depository of their Public Records, for the sole purpose of fatiguing them into compliance with his measures.

He has dissolved Representative Houses repeatedly, for opposing with manly firmness his invasions on the rights of the people.

He has refused for a long time, after such dissolutions, to cause others to be elected, whereby the Legislative Powers, incapable of Annihilation, have returned to the People at large for their exercise; the State remaining in the mean time exposed to all the dangers of invasion from without, and convulsions within.

He has endeavoured to prevent the population of these States; for that purpose obstructing the Laws for Naturalization of Foreigners; refusing to pass others to encourage their migrations hither, and raising the conditions of new Appropriations of Lands.

He has obstructed the Administration of Justice by refusing his Assent to Laws for establishing Judiciary Powers.

He has made Judges dependent on his Will alone for the tenure of their offices, and the amount and payment of their salaries.

He has erected a multitude of New Offices, and sent hither swarms of Officers to harass our people and eat out their substance.

He has kept among us, in times of peace, Standing Armies without the Consent of our legislatures.

He has affected to render the Military independent of and superior to the Civil Power.

He has combined with others to subject us to a jurisdiction foreign to our constitution, and unacknowledged by our laws; giving his Assent to their Acts of pretended Legislation:

For quartering large bodies of armed troops among us:

For protecting them, by a mock Trial from punishment for any Murders which they should commit on the Inhabitants of these States:

For cutting off our Trade with all parts of the world:

For imposing Taxes on us without our Consent:

For depriving us in many cases, of the benefit of Trial by Jury:

For transporting us beyond Seas to be tried for pretended offences:

For abolishing the free System of English Laws in a neighbouring Province, establishing therein an Arbitrary government, and enlarging its Boundaries so as to render it at once an example and fit instrument for introducing the same absolute rule into these Colonies

For taking away our Charters, abolishing our most valuable Laws and altering fundamentally the Forms of our Governments:

For suspending our own Legislatures, and declaring themselves invested with power to legislate for us in all cases whatsoever.

He has abdicated Government here, by declaring us out of his Protection and waging War against us.

He has plundered our seas, ravaged our coasts, burnt our towns, and destroyed the lives of our people.

He is at this time transporting large Armies of foreign Mercenaries to compleat the works of death, desolation, and tyranny, already begun with circumstances of Cruelty & Perfidy scarcely paralleled in the most barbarous ages, and totally unworthy the Head of a civilized nation.

He has constrained our fellow Citizens taken Captive on the high Seas to bear Arms against their Country, to become the executioners of their friends and Brethren, or to fall themselves by their Hands.

He has excited domestic insurrections amongst us, and has endeavoured to bring on the inhabitants of our frontiers, the merciless Indian Savages whose known rule of warfare, is an undistinguished destruction of all ages, sexes and conditions.

In every stage of these Oppressions We have Petitioned for Redress in the most humble terms: Our repeated Petitions have been answered only by repeated injury. A Prince, whose character is thus marked by every act which may define a Tyrant, is unfit to be the ruler of a free people.

Nor have We been wanting in attentions to our British brethren. We have warned them from time to time of attempts by their legislature to extend an unwarrantable jurisdiction over us. We have reminded them of the circumstances of our emigration and settlement here. We have appealed to their native justice and magnanimity, and we have conjured them by the ties of our common kindred to disavow these usurpations, which would inevitably interrupt our connections and correspondence. They too have been deaf to the voice of justice and of consanguinity. We must, therefore, acquiesce in the necessity, which denounces our Separation, and hold them, as we hold the rest of mankind, Enemies in War, in Peace Friends.

We, therefore, the Representatives of the united States of America, in General Congress, Assembled, appealing to the Supreme Judge of the world for the rectitude of our intentions, do, in the Name, and by Authority of the good People of these Colonies, solemnly publish and declare, That these united Colonies are, and of Right ought to be Free and Independent States, that they are Absolved from all Allegiance to the British Crown, and that all political connection between them and the State of Great Britain, is and ought to be totally dissolved; and that as Free and Independent States, they have full Power to levy War, conclude Peace, contract Alliances, establish Commerce, and to do all other Acts and Things which Independent States may of right do. - And for the support of this Declaration, with a firm reliance on the protection of Divine Providence, we mutually pledge to each other our Lives, our Fortunes, and our sacred Honor.

New Hampshire: Josiah Bartlett, William Whipple, Matthew Thornton

Massachusetts: John Hancock, Samuel Adams, John Adams, Robert Treat Paine, Elbridge Gerry

Rhode Island: Stephen Hopkins, William Ellery

Connecticut: Roger Sherman, Samuel Huntington, William Williams, Oliver Wolcott

New York: William Floyd, Philip Livingston, Francis Lewis, Lewis Morris

New Jersey: Richard Stockton, John Witherspoon, Francis Hopkinson, John Hart, Abraham Clark

Pennsylvania: Robert Morris, Benjamin Rush, Benjamin Franklin, John Morton, George Clymer, James Smith, George Taylor, James Wilson, George Ross

Delaware: Caesar Rodney, George Read, Thomas McKean

Maryland: Samuel Chase, William Paca, Thomas Stone, Charles Carroll of Carrollton

Virginia: George Wythe, Richard Henry Lee, Thomas Jefferson, Benjamin Harrison, Thomas Nelson, Jr., Francis Lightfoot Lee, Carter Braxton

North Carolina: William Hooper, Joseph Hewes, John Penn

South Carolina: Edward Rutledge, Thomas Heyward, Jr., Thomas Lynch, Jr., Arthur Middleton

Georgia: Button Gwinnett, Lyman Hall, George Walton

*Note: These transcripts were intended to capture the substance of the document. However, variations in capitalization may exist between the original and this transcription.*

**Transcript of Articles of Confederation (1777)**

To all to whom these Presents shall come, we, the undersigned Delegates of the States affixed to our Names send greeting. Whereas the Delegates of the United States of America in Congress assembled did on the fifteenth day of November in the year of our Lord One Thousand Seven Hundred and Seventy seven, and in the Second Year of the Independence of America agree to certain articles of Confederation and perpetual Union between the States of Newhampshire, Massachusetts-bay, Rhodeisland and Providence Plantations, Connecticut, New York, New Jersey, Pennsylvania, Delaware, Maryland, Virginia, North Carolina, South Carolina, and Georgia in the Words following, viz. "Articles of Confederation and perpetual Union between the States of Newhampshire, Massachusetts-bay, Rhodeisland and Providence Plantations, Connecticut, New York, New Jersey, Pennsylvania, Delaware, Maryland, Virginia, North Carolina, South Carolina, and Georgia.

Article I. The Stile of this confederacy shall be, "The United States of America."

Article II. Each state retains its sovereignty, freedom and independence, and every Power, Jurisdiction and right, which is not by this confederation expressly delegated to the United States, in Congress assembled.

Article III. The said states hereby severally enter into a firm league of friendship with each other, for their common defence, the security of their Liberties, and their mutual and general welfare, binding themselves to assist each other, against all force offered to, or attacks made upon them, or any of them, on account of religion, sovereignty, trade, or any other pretence whatever.

Article IV. The better to secure and perpetuate mutual friendship and intercourse among the people of the different states in this union, the free inhabitants of each of these states, paupers, vagabonds and fugitives from Justice excepted, shall be entitled to all privileges and immunities of free citizens in the several states; and the people of each state shall have free ingress and regress to and from any other state, and shall enjoy therein all the privileges of trade and commerce, subject to the same duties, impositions and restrictions as the inhabitants thereof respectively, provided that such restrictions shall not extend so far as to prevent the removal of property imported into any state, to any other State of which the Owner is an inhabitant; provided also that no imposition, duties or restriction shall be laid by any state, on the property of the united states, or either of them.

If any Person guilty of, or charged with, treason, felony, or other high misdemeanor in any state, shall flee from Justice, and be found in any of the united states, he shall upon demand of the Governor or executive power of the state from which he fled, be delivered up, and removed to the state having jurisdiction of his offence.

Full faith and credit shall be given in each of these states to the records, acts and judicial proceedings of the courts and magistrates of every other state.

Article V. For the more convenient management of the general interests of the united states, delegates shall be annually appointed in such manner as the legislature of each state shall direct, to meet in Congress on the first Monday in November, in every year, with a power reserved to each state to recall its delegates, or any of them, at any time within the year, and to send others in their stead, for the remainder of the Year.

No State shall be represented in Congress by less than two, nor by more than seven Members; and no person shall be capable of being delegate for more than three years, in any term of six years; nor shall any person, being a delegate, be capable of holding any office under the united states, for which he, or another for his benefit receives any salary, fees or emolument of any kind.

Each State shall maintain its own delegates in a meeting of the states, and while they act as members of the committee of the states.

In determining questions in the united states, in Congress assembled, each state shall have one vote.

Freedom of speech and debate in Congress shall not be impeached or questioned in any Court, or place out of Congress, and the members of congress shall be protected in their persons from arrests and imprisonments, during the time of their going to and from, and attendance on congress, except for treason, felony, or breach of the peace.

Article VI. No State, without the Consent of the united States, in congress assembled, shall send any embassy to, or receive any embassy from, or enter into any conferrence, agreement, alliance, or treaty, with any King prince or state; nor shall any person holding any office of profit or trust under the united states, or any of them, accept of any present, emolument, office, or title of any kind whatever, from any king, prince, or foreign state; nor shall the united states, in congress assembled, or any of them, grant any title of nobility.

No two or more states shall enter into any treaty, confederation, or alliance whatever between them, without the consent of the united states, in congress assembled, specifying accurately the purposes for which the same is to be entered into, and how long it shall continue.

No State shall lay any imposts or duties, which may interfere with any stipulations in treaties, entered into by the united States in congress assembled, with any king, prince, or State, in pursuance of any treaties already proposed by congress, to the courts of France and Spain.

No vessels of war shall be kept up in time of peace, by any state, except such number only, as shall be deemed necessary by the united states, in congress assembled, for the defence of such state, or its trade; nor shall any body of forces be kept up, by any state, in time of peace, except such number only as, in the judgment of the united states, in congress assembled, shall be deemed requisite to garrison the forts necessary for the defence of such state; but every state shall always keep up a well regulated and disciplined militia, sufficiently armed and accounted, and shall provide and constantly have ready for use, in public stores, a due number of field pieces and tents, and a proper quantity of arms, ammunition, and camp equipage.

No State shall engage in any war without the consent of the united States in congress assembled, unless such State be actually invaded by enemies, or shall have received certain advice of a resolution being formed by some nation of Indians to invade such State, and the danger is so imminent as not to admit of a delay till the united states in congress assembled, can be consulted: nor shall any state grant commissions to any ships or vessels of war, nor letters of marque or reprisal, except it be after a declaration of war by the united states in congress assembled, and then only against the kingdom or State, and the subjects thereof, against which war has been so declared, and under such regulations as shall be established by the united states in congress assembled, unless such state be infested by pirates, in which case vessels of war may be fitted out for that occasion, and kept so long as the danger shall continue, or until the united states in congress assembled shall determine otherwise.

Article VII. When land forces are raised by any state, for the common defence, all officers of or under the rank of colonel, shall be appointed by the legislature of each state respectively by whom such forces shall be raised, or in such manner as such state shall direct, and all vacancies shall be filled up by the state which first made appointment.

Article VIII. All charges of war, and all other expenses that shall be incurred for the common defence or general welfare, and allowed by the united states in congress assembled, shall be defrayed out of a common treasury, which shall be supplied by the several states, in proportion to the value of all land within each state, granted to or surveyed for any Person, as such land and the buildings and improvements thereon shall be estimated, according to such mode as the united states, in congress assembled, shall, from time to time, direct and appoint. The taxes for paying that proportion shall be laid and levied by the authority and direction of the legislatures of the several states within the time agreed upon by the united states in congress assembled.

Article IX. The united states, in congress assembled, shall have the sole and exclusive right and power of determining on peace and war, except in the cases mentioned in the sixth article - of sending and receiving ambassadors - entering into treaties and alliances, provided that no treaty of commerce shall be made, whereby the legislative power of the respective states shall be restrained from imposing such imposts and duties on foreigners, as their own people are subjected to, or from prohibiting the exportation or importation of any species of goods or commodities whatsoever - of establishing rules for deciding, in all cases, what captures on land or water shall be legal, and in what manner prizes taken by land or naval forces in the service of the united Sates, shall be divided or appropriated - of granting letters of marque and reprisal in times of peace - appointing courts for the trial of piracies and felonies committed on the high seas; and establishing courts; for receiving and determining finally appeals in all cases of captures; provided that no member of congress shall be appointed a judge of any of the said courts.

The united states, in congress assembled, shall also be the last resort on appeal, in all disputes and differences now subsisting, or that hereafter may arise between two or more states concerning boundary, jurisdiction, or any other cause whatever; which authority shall always be exercised in the manner following. Whenever the legislative or executive authority, or lawful agent of any state in controversy with another, shall present a petition to congress, stating the matter in question, and praying for a hearing, notice thereof shall be given, by order of congress, to the legislative or executive authority of the other state in controversy, and a day assigned for the appearance of the parties by their lawful agents, who shall then be directed to appoint, by joint consent, commissioners or judges to constitute a court for hearing and determining the matter in question: but if they cannot agree, congress shall name three persons out of each of the united states, and from the list of such persons each party shall alternately strike out one, the petitioners beginning, until the number shall be reduced to thirteen; and from that number not less than seven, nor more than nine names, as congress shall direct, shall, in the presence of congress, be drawn out by lot, and the persons whose names shall be so drawn, or any five of them, shall be commissioners or judges, to hear and finally determine the controversy, so always as a major part of the judges, who shall hear the cause, shall agree in the determination: and if either party shall neglect to attend at the day appointed, without showing reasons which congress shall judge sufficient, or being present, shall refuse to strike, the congress shall proceed to nominate three persons out of each State, and the secretary of congress shall strike in behalf of such party absent or refusing; and the judgment and sentence of the court, to be appointed in the manner before prescribed, shall be final and conclusive; and if any of the parties shall refuse to submit to the authority of such court, or to appear or defend their claim or cause, the court shall nevertheless proceed to pronounce sentence, or judgment, which shall in like manner be final and decisive; the judgment or sentence and other proceedings being in either case transmitted to congress, and lodged among the acts of congress, for the security of the parties concerned: provided that every commissioner, before he sits in judgment, shall take an oath to be administered by one of the judges of the supreme or superior court of the State where the cause shall be tried, "well and truly to hear and determine the matter in question, according to the best of his judgment, without favour, affection, or hope of reward: "provided, also, that no State shall be deprived of territory for the benefit of the united states.

All controversies concerning the private right of soil claimed under different grants of two or more states, whose jurisdictions as they may respect such lands, and the states which passed such grants are adjusted, the said grants or either of them being at the same time claimed to have originated antecedent to such settlement of jurisdiction, shall, on the petition of either party to the congress of the united states, be finally determined, as near as may be, in the same manner as is before prescribed for deciding disputes respecting territorial jurisdiction between different states.

The united states, in congress assembled, shall also have the sole and exclusive right and power of regulating the alloy and value of coin struck by their own authority, or by that of the respective states - fixing the standard of weights and measures throughout the united states - regulating the trade and managing all affairs with the Indians, not members of any of the states; provided that the legislative right of any state, within its own limits, be not infringed or violated - establishing and regulating post-offices from one state to another, throughout all the united states, and exacting such postage on the papers passing through the same, as may be requisite to defray the expenses of the said office - appointing all officers of the land forces in the service of the united States, excepting regimental officers - appointing all the officers of the naval forces, and commissioning all officers whatever in the service of the united states; making rules for the government and regulation of the said land and naval forces, and directing their operations.

The united States, in congress assembled, shall have authority to appoint a committee, to sit in the recess of congress, to be denominated, "A Committee of the States," and to consist of one delegate from each State; and to appoint such other committees and civil officers as may be necessary for managing the general affairs of the united states under their direction - to appoint one of their number to preside; provided that no person be allowed to serve in the office of president more than one year in any term of three years; to ascertain the necessary sums of money to be raised for the service of the united states, and to appropriate and apply the same for defraying the public expenses; to borrow money or emit bills on the credit of the united states, transmitting every half year to the respective states an account of the sums of money so borrowed or emitted, - to build and equip a navy - to agree upon the number of land forces, and to make requisitions from each state for its quota, in proportion to the number of white inhabitants in such state, which requisition shall be binding; and thereupon the legislature of each state shall appoint the regimental officers, raise the men, and clothe, arm, and equip them, in a soldier-like manner, at the expense of the united states; and the officers and men so clothed, armed, and equipped, shall march to the place appointed, and within the time agreed on by the united states, in congress assembled; but if the united states, in congress assembled, shall, on consideration of circumstances, judge proper that any state should not raise men, or should raise a smaller number than its quota, and that any other state should raise a greater number of men than the quota thereof, such extra number shall be raised, officered, clothed, armed, and equipped in the same manner as the quota of such state, unless the legislature of such state shall judge that such extra number cannot be safely spared out of the same, in which case they shall raise, officer, clothe, arm, and equip, as many of such extra number as they judge can be safely spared. And the officers and men so clothed, armed, and equipped, shall march to the place appointed, and within the time agreed on by the united states in congress assembled.

The united states, in congress assembled, shall never engage in a war, nor grant letters of marque and reprisal in time of peace, nor enter into any treaties or alliances, nor coin money, nor regulate the value thereof nor ascertain the sums and expenses necessary for the defence and welfare of the united states, or any of them, nor emit bills, nor borrow money on the credit of the united states, nor appropriate money, nor agree upon the number of vessels of war to be built or purchased, or the number of land or sea forces to be raised, nor appoint a commander in chief of the army or navy, unless nine states assent to the same, nor shall a question on any other point, except for adjourning from day to day, be determined, unless by the votes of a majority of the united states in congress assembled.

The congress of the united states shall have power to adjourn to any time within the year, and to any place within the united states, so that no period of adjournment be for a longer duration than the space of six Months, and shall publish the Journal of their proceedings monthly, except such parts thereof relating to treaties, alliances, or military operations, as in their judgment require secrecy; and the yeas and nays of the delegates of each State, on any question, shall be entered on the Journal, when it is desired by any delegate; and the delegates of a State, or any of them, at his or their request, shall be furnished with a transcript of the said Journal, except such parts as are above excepted, to lay before the legislatures of the several states.

Article X. The committee of the states, or any nine of them, shall be authorized to execute, in the recess of congress, such of the powers of congress as the united states, in congress assembled, by the consent of nine states, shall, from time to time, think expedient to vest them with; provided that no power be delegated to the said committee, for the exercise of which, by the articles of confederation, the voice of nine states, in the congress of the united states assembled, is requisite.

Article XI. Canada acceding to this confederation, and joining in the measures of the united states, shall be admitted into, and entitled to all the advantages of this union: but no other colony shall be admitted into the same, unless such admission be agreed to by nine states.

Article XII. All bills of credit emitted, monies borrowed, and debts contracted by or under the authority of congress, before the assembling of the united states, in pursuance of the present confederation, shall be deemed and considered as a charge against the united States, for payment and satisfaction whereof the said united states and the public faith are hereby solemnly pledged.

Article XIII. Every State shall abide by the determinations of the united states, in congress assembled, on all questions which by this confederation are submitted to them. And the Articles of this confederation shall be inviolably observed by every state, and the union shall be perpetual; nor shall any alteration at any time hereafter be made in any of them, unless such alteration be agreed to in a congress of the united states, and be afterwards con-firmed by the legislatures of every state.

And Whereas it hath pleased the Great Governor of the World to incline the hearts of the legislatures we respectively represent in congress, to approve of, and to authorize us to ratify the said articles of confederation and perpetual union, Know Ye, that we, the undersigned delegates, by virtue of the power and authority to us given for that purpose, do, by these presents, in the name and in behalf of our respective constituents, fully and entirely ratify and confirm each and every of the said articles of confederation and perpetual union, and all and singular the matters and things therein contained. And we do further solemnly plight and engage the faith of our respective constituents, that they shall abide by the determinations of the united states in congress assembled, on all questions, which by the said confederation are submitted to them. And that the articles thereof shall be inviolably observed by the states we respectively represent, and that the union shall be perpetual. In Witness whereof, we have hereunto set our hands, in Congress. Done at Philadelphia, in the State of Pennsylvania, the ninth Day of July, in the Year of our Lord one Thousand seven Hundred and Seventy eight, and in the third year of the Independence of America.

*Note: The following text is a transcription of the Constitution as it was inscribed by Jacob Shallus on parchment (the document on display in the Rotunda at the National Archives Museum.) The spelling and punctuation reflect the original.*

## Consitution of the United States of America

We the People of the United States, in Order to form a more perfect Union, establish Justice, insure domestic Tranquility, provide for the common defence, promote the general Welfare, and secure the Blessings of Liberty to ourselves and our Posterity, do ordain and establish this Constitution for the United States of America.

## Article. I.

Section. 1.

All legislative Powers herein granted shall be vested in a Congress of the United States, which shall consist of a Senate and House of Representatives.

Section. 2.

The House of Representatives shall be composed of Members chosen every second Year by the People of the several States, and the Electors in each State shall have the Qualifications requisite for Electors of the most numerous Branch of the State Legislature.

No Person shall be a Representative who shall not have attained to the Age of twenty five Years, and been seven Years a Citizen of the United States, and who shall not, when elected, be an Inhabitant of that State in which he shall be chosen.

Representatives and direct Taxes shall be apportioned among the several States which may be included within this Union, according to their respective Numbers, which shall be determined by adding to the whole Number of free Persons, including those bound to Service for a Term of Years, and excluding Indians not taxed, three fifths of all other Persons. The actual Enumeration shall be made within three Years after the first Meeting of the Congress of the United States, and within every subsequent Term of ten Years, in such Manner as they shall by Law direct. The Number of Representatives shall not exceed one for every thirty Thousand, but each

State shall have at Least one Representative; and until such enumeration shall be made, the State of New Hampshire shall be entitled to chuse three, Massachusetts eight, Rhode-Island and Providence Plantations one, Connecticut five, New-York six, New Jersey four, Pennsylvania eight, Delaware one, Maryland six, Virginia ten, North Carolina five, South Carolina five, and Georgia three.

When vacancies happen in the Representation from any State, the Executive Authority thereof shall issue Writs of Election to fill such Vacancies.

The House of Representatives shall chuse their Speaker and other Officers; and shall have the sole Power of Impeachment.

Section. 3.

The Senate of the United States shall be composed of two Senators from each State, chosen by the Legislature thereof, for six Years; and each Senator shall have one Vote.

Immediately after they shall be assembled in Consequence of the first Election, they shall be divided as equally as may be into three Classes. The Seats of the Senators of the first Class shall be vacated at the Expiration of the second Year, of the second Class at the Expiration of the fourth Year, and of the third Class at the Expiration of the sixth Year, so that one third may be chosen every second Year; and if Vacancies happen by Resignation, or otherwise, during the Recess of the Legislature of any State, the Executive thereof may make temporary Appointments until the next Meeting of the Legislature, which shall then fill such Vacancies.

No Person shall be a Senator who shall not have attained to the Age of thirty Years, and been nine Years a Citizen of the United States, and who shall not, when elected, be an Inhabitant of that State for which he shall be chosen.

The Vice President of the United States shall be President of the Senate, but shall have no Vote, unless they be equally divided.

The Senate shall chuse their other Officers, and also a President pro tempore, in the Absence of the Vice President, or when he shall exercise the Office of President of the United States.

The Senate shall have the sole Power to try all Impeachments. When sitting for that Purpose, they shall be on Oath or Affirmation. When the President of the United States is tried, the Chief Justice shall preside: And no Person shall be convicted without the Concurrence of two thirds of the Members present.

Judgment in Cases of Impeachment shall not extend further than to removal from Office, and disqualification to hold and enjoy any Office of honor, Trust or Profit under the United States: but the Party convicted shall nevertheless be liable and subject to Indictment, Trial, Judgment and Punishment, according to Law.

Section. 4.

The Times, Places and Manner of holding Elections for Senators and Representatives, shall be prescribed in each State by the Legislature thereof; but the Congress may at any time by Law make or alter such Regulations, except as to the Places of chusing Senators.

The Congress shall assemble at least once in every Year, and such Meeting shall be on the first Monday in December, unless they shall by Law appoint a different Day.

Section. 5.

Each House shall be the Judge of the Elections, Returns and Qualifications of its own Members, and a Majority of each shall constitute a Quorum to do Business; but a smaller Number may adjourn from day to day, and may be authorized to compel the Attendance of absent Members, in such Manner, and under such Penalties as each House may provide.

Each House may determine the Rules of its Proceedings, punish its Members for disorderly Behaviour, and, with the Concurrence of two thirds, expel a Member.

Each House shall keep a Journal of its Proceedings, and from time to time publish the same, excepting such Parts as may in their Judgment require Secrecy; and the Yeas and Nays of the Members of either House on any question shall, at the Desire of one fifth of those Present, be entered on the Journal.

Neither House, during the Session of Congress, shall, without the Consent of the other, adjourn for more than three days, nor to any other Place than that in which the two Houses shall be sitting.

Section. 6.

The Senators and Representatives shall receive a Compensation for their Services, to be ascertained by Law, and paid out of the Treasury of the United States. They shall in all Cases, except Treason, Felony and Breach of the Peace, be privileged from Arrest during their Attendance at the Session of their respective Houses, and in going to and returning from the same; and for any Speech or Debate in either House, they shall not be questioned in any other Place.

No Senator or Representative shall, during the Time for which he was elected, be appointed to any civil Office under the Authority of the United States, which shall have been created, or the Emoluments whereof shall have been encreased during such time; and no Person holding any Office under the United States, shall be a Member of either House during his Continuance in Office.

Section. 7.

All Bills for raising Revenue shall originate in the House of Representatives; but the Senate may propose or concur with Amendments as on other Bills.

Every Bill which shall have passed the House of Representatives and the Senate, shall, before it become a Law, be presented to the President of the United States; If he approve he shall sign it, but if not he shall return it, with his Objections to that House in which it shall have originated, who shall enter the Objections at large on their Journal, and proceed to reconsider it. If after such Reconsideration two thirds of that House shall agree to pass the Bill, it shall be sent, together with the Objections, to the other House, by which it shall likewise be reconsidered, and if approved by two thirds of that House, it shall become a Law. But in all such Cases the Votes of both Houses shall be determined by yeas and Nays, and the Names of the Persons voting for and against the Bill shall be entered on the Journal of each House respectively. If any Bill shall not be returned by the President within ten Days (Sundays excepted) after it shall have been presented to him, the Same shall be a Law, in like Manner as if he had signed it, unless the Congress by their Adjournment prevent its Return, in which Case it shall not be a Law.

Every Order, Resolution, or Vote to which the Concurrence of the Senate and House of Representatives may be necessary (except on a question of Adjournment) shall be presented to the President of the United States; and before the Same shall take Effect, shall be approved by him, or being disapproved by him, shall be repassed by two thirds of the Senate and House of Representatives, according to the Rules and Limitations prescribed in the Case of a Bill.

Section. 8.

The Congress shall have Power To lay and collect Taxes, Duties, Imposts and Excises, to pay the Debts and provide for the common Defence and general Welfare of the United States; but all Duties, Imposts and Excises shall be uniform throughout the United States;

To borrow Money on the credit of the United States;

To regulate Commerce with foreign Nations, and among the several States, and with the Indian Tribes;

To establish an uniform Rule of Naturalization, and uniform Laws on the subject of Bankruptcies throughout the United States;

To coin Money, regulate the Value thereof, and of foreign Coin, and fix the Standard of Weights and Measures;

To provide for the Punishment of counterfeiting the Securities and current Coin of the United States;

To establish Post Offices and post Roads;

To promote the Progress of Science and useful Arts, by securing for limited Times to Authors and Inventors the exclusive Right to their respective Writings and Discoveries;

To constitute Tribunals inferior to the supreme Court;

To define and punish Piracies and Felonies committed on the high Seas, and Offences against the Law of Nations;

To declare War, grant Letters of Marque and Reprisal, and make Rules concerning Captures on Land and Water;

To raise and support Armies, but no Appropriation of Money to that Use shall be for a longer Term than two Years;

To provide and maintain a Navy;

To make Rules for the Government and Regulation of the land and naval Forces;

To provide for calling forth the Militia to execute the Laws of the Union, suppress Insurrections and repel Invasions;

To provide for organizing, arming, and disciplining, the Militia, and for governing such Part of them as may be employed in the Service of the United States, reserving to the States respectively, the Appointment of the Officers, and the Authority of training the Militia according to the discipline prescribed by Congress;

To exercise exclusive Legislation in all Cases whatsoever, over such District (not exceeding ten Miles square) as may, by Cession of particular States, and the Acceptance of Congress, become the Seat of the Government of the United States, and to exercise like Authority over all Places purchased by the Consent of the Legislature of the State in which the Same shall be, for the Erection of Forts, Magazines, Arsenals, dock-Yards, and other needful Buildings; - And

To make all Laws which shall be necessary and proper for carrying into Execution the foregoing Powers, and all other Powers vested by this Constitution in the Government of the United States, or in any Department or Officer thereof.

Section. 9.

The Migration or Importation of such Persons as any of the States now existing shall think proper to admit, shall not be prohibited by the Congress prior to the Year one thousand eight hundred and eight, but a Tax or duty may be imposed on such Importation, not exceeding ten dollars for each Person.

The Privilege of the Writ of Habeas Corpus shall not be suspended, unless when in Cases of Rebellion or Invasion the public Safety may require it.

No Bill of Attainder or ex post facto Law shall be passed.

No Capitation, or other direct, Tax shall be laid, unless in Proportion to the Census or enumeration herein before directed to be taken.

No Tax or Duty shall be laid on Articles exported from any State.

No Preference shall be given by any Regulation of Commerce or Revenue to the Ports of one State over those of another: nor shall Vessels bound to, or from, one State, be obliged to enter, clear, or pay Duties in another.

No Money shall be drawn from the Treasury, but in Consequence of Appropriations made by Law; and a regular Statement and Account of the Receipts and Expenditures of all public Money shall be published from time to time.

No Title of Nobility shall be granted by the United States: And no Person holding any Office of Profit or Trust under them, shall, without the Consent of the Congress, accept of any present, Emolument, Office, or Title, of any kind whatever, from any King, Prince, or foreign State.

Section. 10.

No State shall enter into any Treaty, Alliance, or Confederation; grant Letters of Marque and Reprisal; coin Money; emit Bills of Credit; make any Thing but gold and silver Coin a Tender in Payment of Debts; pass any Bill of Attainder, ex post facto Law, or Law impairing the Obligation of Contracts, or grant any Title of Nobility.

No State shall, without the Consent of the Congress, lay any Imposts or Duties on Imports or Exports, except what may be absolutely necessary for executing it's inspection Laws: and the net Produce of all Duties and Imposts, laid by any State on Imports or Exports, shall be for the Use of the Treasury of the United States; and all such Laws shall be subject to the Revision and Controul of the Congress.

No State shall, without the Consent of Congress, lay any Duty of Tonnage, keep Troops, or Ships of War in time of Peace, enter into any Agreement or Compact with another State, or with a foreign Power, or engage in War, unless actually invaded, or in such imminent Danger as will not admit of delay.

## Article. II.

Section. 1.

The executive Power shall be vested in a President of the United States of America. He shall hold his Office during the Term of four Years, and, together with the Vice President, chosen for the same Term, be elected, as follows

Each State shall appoint, in such Manner as the Legislature thereof may direct, a Number of Electors, equal to the whole Number of Senators and Representatives to which the State may be entitled in the Congress: but no Senator or Representative, or Person holding an Office of Trust or Profit under the United States, shall be appointed an Elector.

The Electors shall meet in their respective States, and vote by Ballot for two Persons, of whom one at least shall not be an Inhabitant of the same State with themselves. And they shall make a List of all the Persons voted for, and of the Number of Votes for each; which List they shall sign and certify, and transmit sealed to the Seat of the Government of the United States, directed to the President of the Senate. The President of the Senate shall, in the Presence of the Senate and House of Representatives, open all the Certificates, and the Votes shall then be counted. The Person having the greatest Number of Votes shall be the President, if such Number be a Majority of the whole Number of Electors appointed; and if there be more than one who have such Majority, and have an equal Number of Votes, then the House of Representatives shall immediately chuse by Ballot one of them for President; and if no Person have a Majority, then from the five highest on the List the said House shall in like Manner chuse the President. But in chusing the President, the Votes shall be taken by States, the Representation from each State having one Vote; A quorum for this Purpose shall consist of a Member or Members from two thirds of the States, and a Majority of all the States shall be necessary to a Choice. In every Case, after the Choice of the President, the Person having the greatest Number of Votes of the Electors shall be the Vice President. But if there should remain two or more who have equal Votes, the Senate shall chuse from them by Ballot the Vice President.

The Congress may determine the Time of chusing the Electors, and the Day on which they shall give their Votes; which Day shall be the same throughout the United States.

No Person except a natural born Citizen, or a Citizen of the United States, at the time of the Adoption of this Constitution, shall be eligible to the Office of President; neither shall any Person be eligible to that Office who shall not have attained to the Age of thirty five Years, and been fourteen Years a Resident within the United States.

In Case of the Removal of the President from Office, or of his Death, Resignation, or Inability to discharge the Powers and Duties of the said Office, the Same shall devolve on the Vice President, and the Congress may by Law provide for the Case of Removal, Death, Resignation or Inability, both of the President and Vice President, declaring what Officer shall then act as President, and such Officer shall act accordingly, until the Disability be removed, or a President shall be elected.

The President shall, at stated Times, receive for his Services, a Compensation, which shall neither be encreased nor diminished during the Period for which he shall have been elected, and he shall not receive within that Period any other Emolument from the United States, or any of them.

Before he enter on the Execution of his Office, he shall take the following Oath or Affirmation: - "I do solemnly swear (or affirm) that I will faithfully execute the Office of President of the United States, and will to the best of my Ability, preserve, protect and defend the Constitution of the United States."

Section. 2.

The President shall be Commander in Chief of the Army and Navy of the United States, and of the Militia of the several States, when called into the actual Service of the United States; he may require the Opinion, in writing, of the principal Officer in each of the executive Departments, upon any Subject relating to the Duties of their respective Offices, and he shall have Power to grant Reprieves and Pardons for Offences against the United States, except in Cases of Impeachment.

He shall have Power, by and with the Advice and Consent of the Senate, to make Treaties, provided two thirds of the Senators present concur; and he shall nominate, and by and with the Advice and Consent of the Senate, shall appoint Ambassadors, other public Ministers and Consuls, Judges of the supreme Court, and all other Officers of the United States, whose Appointments are not herein otherwise provided for, and which shall be established by Law: but the Congress may by Law vest the Appointment of such inferior Officers, as they think proper, in the President alone, in the Courts of Law, or in the Heads of Departments.

The President shall have Power to fill up all Vacancies that may happen during the Recess of the Senate, by granting Commissions which shall expire at the End of their next Session.

Section. 3.

He shall from time to time give to the Congress Information of the State of the Union, and recommend to their Consideration such Measures as he shall judge necessary and expedient; he may, on extraordinary Occasions, convene both Houses, or either of them, and in Case of Disagreement between them, with Respect to the Time of Adjournment, he may adjourn them to such Time as he shall think proper; he shall receive Ambassadors and other public Ministers; he shall take Care that the Laws be faithfully executed, and shall Commission all the Officers of the United States.

Section. 4.

The President, Vice President and all civil Officers of the United States, shall be removed from Office on Impeachment for, and Conviction of, Treason, Bribery, or other high Crimes and Misdemeanors.

**Article III.**

Section. 1.

The judicial Power of the United States, shall be vested in one supreme Court, and in such inferior Courts as the Congress may from time to time ordain and establish. The Judges, both of the supreme and inferior Courts, shall hold their Offices during good Behaviour, and shall, at stated Times, receive for their Services, a Compensation, which shall not be diminished during their Continuance in Office.

Section. 2.

The judicial Power shall extend to all Cases, in Law and Equity, arising under this Constitution, the Laws of the United States, and Treaties made, or which shall be made, under their Authority; - to all Cases affecting Ambassadors, other public Ministers and Consuls; - to all Cases of admiralty and maritime Jurisdiction; - to Controversies to which the United States shall be a Party; - to Controversies between two or more States; - between a State and Citizens of another State, - between Citizens of different States, - between Citizens of the same State claiming Lands under Grants of different States, and between a State, or the Citizens thereof, and foreign States, Citizens or Subjects.

In all Cases affecting Ambassadors, other public Ministers and Consuls, and those in which a State shall be Party, the supreme Court shall have original Jurisdiction. In all the other Cases before mentioned, the supreme Court shall have appellate Jurisdiction, both as to Law and Fact, with such Exceptions, and under such Regulations as the Congress shall make.

The Trial of all Crimes, except in Cases of Impeachment, shall be by Jury; and such Trial shall be held in the State where the said Crimes shall have been committed; but when not committed within any State, the Trial shall be at such Place or Places as the Congress may by Law have directed.

Section. 3.

Treason against the United States, shall consist only in levying War against them, or in adhering to their Enemies, giving them Aid and Comfort. No Person shall be convicted of Treason unless on the Testimony of two Witnesses to the same overt Act, or on Confession in open Court.

The Congress shall have Power to declare the Punishment of Treason, but no Attainder of Treason shall work Corruption of Blood, or Forfeiture except during the Life of the Person attainted.

**Article. IV.**

Section. 1.

Full Faith and Credit shall be given in each State to the public Acts, Records, and judicial Proceedings of every other State. And the Congress may by general Laws prescribe the Manner in which such Acts, Records and Proceedings shall be proved, and the Effect thereof.

Section. 2.

The Citizens of each State shall be entitled to all Privileges and Immunities of Citizens in the several States.

A Person charged in any State with Treason, Felony, or other Crime, who shall flee from Justice, and be found in another State, shall on Demand of the executive Authority of the State from which he fled, be delivered up, to be removed to the State having Jurisdiction of the Crime.

No Person held to Service or Labour in one State, under the Laws thereof, escaping into another, shall, in Consequence of any Law or Regulation therein, be discharged from such Service or Labour, but shall be delivered up on Claim of the Party to whom such Service or Labour may be due.

Section. 3.

New States may be admitted by the Congress into this Union; but no new State shall be formed or erected within the Jurisdiction of any other State; nor any State be formed by the Junction of two or more States, or Parts of States, without the Consent of the Legislatures of the States concerned as well as of the Congress.

The Congress shall have Power to dispose of and make all needful Rules and Regulations respecting the Territory or other Property belonging to the United States; and nothing in this Constitution shall be so construed as to Prejudice any Claims of the United States, or of any particular State.

Section. 4.

The United States shall guarantee to every State in this Union a Republican Form of Government, and shall protect each of them against Invasion; and on Application of the Legislature, or of the Executive (when the Legislature cannot be convened), against domestic Violence.

**Article. V.**

The Congress, whenever two thirds of both Houses shall deem it necessary, shall propose Amendments to this Constitution, or, on the Application of the Legislatures of two thirds of the several States, shall call a Convention for proposing Amendments, which, in either Case, shall be valid to all

Intents and Purposes, as Part of this Constitution, when ratified by the Legislatures of three fourths of the several States, or by Conventions in three fourths thereof, as the one or the other Mode of Ratification may be proposed by the Congress; Provided that no Amendment which may be made prior to the Year One thousand eight hundred and eight shall in any Manner affect the first and fourth Clauses in the Ninth Section of the first Article; and that no State, without its Consent, shall be deprived of its equal Suffrage in the Senate.

## Article. VI.

All Debts contracted and Engagements entered into, before the Adoption of this Constitution, shall be as valid against the United States under this Constitution, as under the Confederation.

This Constitution, and the Laws of the United States which shall be made in Pursuance thereof; and all Treaties made, or which shall be made, under the Authority of the United States, shall be the supreme Law of the Land; and the Judges in every State shall be bound thereby, any Thing in the Constitution or Laws of any State to the Contrary notwithstanding.

The Senators and Representatives before mentioned, and the Members of the several State Legislatures, and all executive and judicial Officers, both of the United States and of the several States, shall be bound by Oath or Affirmation, to support this Constitution; but no religious Test shall ever be required as a Qualification to any Office or public Trust under the United States.

## Article. VII.

The Ratification of the Conventions of nine States, shall be sufficient for the Establishment of this Constitution between the States so ratifying the Same.

The Word, "the," being interlined between the seventh and eighth Lines of the first Page, The Word "Thirty" being partly written on an Erazure in the fifteenth Line of the first Page, The Words "is tried" being interlined between the thirty second and thirty third Lines of the first Page and the Word "the" being interlined between the forty third and forty fourth Lines of the second Page.

Attest William Jackson Secretary

Done in Convention by the Unanimous Consent of the States present the Seventeenth Day of September in the Year of our Lord one thousand seven hundred and Eighty seven and of the Independance of the United States of America the Twelfth In witness whereof We have hereunto subscribed our Names,

G$^o$. Washington, Presidt and deputy from Virginia

Delaware - Geo: Read, Gunning Bedford jun, John Dickinson, Richard Bassett, Jaco: Broom

Maryland - James McHenry, Dan of St Thos. Jenifer, Danl. Carroll

Virginia - John Blair, James Madison Jr.

North Carolina - Wm. Blount, Richd. Dobbs Spaight, Hu Williamson

South Carolina - J. Rutledge, Charles Cotesworth Pinckney, Charles Pinckney, Pierce Butler

Georgia - William Few, Abr Baldwin

New Hampshire - John Langdon, Nicholas Gilman

Massachusetts - Nathaniel Gorham, Rufus King

Connecticut - Wm. Saml. Johnson, Roger Sherman

New York - Alexander Hamilton

New Jersey - Wil: Livingston, David Brearley, Wm. Paterson, Jona: Dayton

Pennsylvania - B Franklin, Thomas Mifflin, Robt. Morris, Geo. Clymer, Thos. FitzSimons, Jared Ingersoll, James Wilson, Gouv Morris

*Note: The following text is a transcription of the enrolled original of the Joint Resolution of Congress proposing the Bill of Rights, which is on permanent display in the Rotunda at the National Archives Museum. The spelling and punctuation reflects the original.*

On September 25, 1789, the First Congress of the United States proposed 12 amendments to the Constitution. The 1789 Joint Resolution of Congress proposing the amendments is on display in the Rotunda in the National Archives Museum. Ten of the proposed 12 amendments were ratified by three-fourths of the state legislatures on December 15, 1791. The ratified Articles (Articles 3–12) constitute the first 10 amendments of the Constitution, or the U.S. Bill of Rights. In 1992, 203 years after it was proposed, Article 2 was ratified as the 27th Amendment to the Constitution. Article 1 was never ratified.

**Transcription of the 1789 Joint Resolution of Congress Proposing 12 Amendments to the U.S. Constitution**

Congress of the United States begun and held at the City of New-York, on Wednesday the fourth of March, one thousand seven hundred and eighty nine.

THE Conventions of a number of the States, having at the time of their adopting the Constitution, expressed a desire, in order to prevent misconstruction or abuse of its powers, that further declaratory and restrictive clauses should be added: And as extending the ground of public confidence in the Government, will best ensure the beneficent ends of its institution.

RESOLVED by the Senate and House of Representatives of the United States of America, in Congress assembled, two thirds of both Houses concurring, that the following Articles be proposed to the Legislatures of the several States, as amendments to the Constitution of the United States, all, or any of which Articles, when ratified by three fourths of the said Legislatures, to be valid to all intents and purposes, as part of the said Constitution; viz.

ARTICLES in addition to, and Amendment of the Constitution of the United States of America, proposed by Congress, and ratified by the Legislatures of the several States, pursuant to the fifth Article of the original Constitution.

Article the first... After the first enumeration required by the first article of the Constitution, there shall be one Representative for every thirty thousand, until the number shall amount to one hundred, after which the proportion shall be so regulated by Congress, that there shall be not less than one hundred Representatives, nor less than one Representative for every forty thousand persons, until the number of Representatives shall amount to two hundred; after which the proportion shall be so regulated by Congress, that there shall not be less than two hundred Representatives, nor more than one Representative for every fifty thousand persons.

Article the second... No law, varying the compensation for the services of the Senators and Representatives, shall take effect, until an election of Representatives shall have intervened.

Article the third... Congress shall make no law respecting an establishment of religion, or prohibiting the free exercise thereof; or abridging the freedom of speech, or of the press; or the right of the people peaceably to assemble, and to petition the Government for a redress of grievances.

Article the fourth... A well regulated Militia, being necessary to the security of a free State, the right of the people to keep and bear Arms, shall not be infringed.

Article the fifth... No Soldier shall, in time of peace be quartered in any house, without the consent of the Owner, nor in time of war, but in a manner to be prescribed by law.

Article the sixth... The right of the people to be secure in their persons, houses, papers, and effects, against unreasonable searches and seizures, shall not be violated, and no Warrants shall issue, but upon probable cause, supported by Oath or affirmation, and particularly describing the place to be searched, and the persons or things to be seized.

Article the seventh... No person shall be held to answer for a capital, or otherwise infamous crime, unless on a presentment or indictment of a Grand Jury, except in cases arising in the land or naval forces, or in the Militia, when in actual service in time of War or public danger; nor shall any person be subject for the same offence to be twice put in jeopardy of life or limb; nor shall be compelled in any criminal case to be a witness against himself, nor be deprived of life, liberty, or property, without due process of law; nor shall private property be taken for public use, without just compensation.

Article the eighth... In all criminal prosecutions, the accused shall enjoy the right to a speedy and public trial, by an impartial jury of the State and district wherein the crime shall have been committed, which district shall have been previously ascertained by law, and to be informed of the nature and cause of the accusation; to be confronted with the witnesses against him; to have compulsory process for obtaining witnesses in his favor, and to have the Assistance of Counsel for his defence.

Article the ninth... In suits at common law, where the value in controversy shall exceed twenty dollars, the right of trial by jury shall be preserved, and no fact tried by a jury, shall be otherwise re-examined in any Court of the United States, than according to the rules of the common law.

Article the tenth... Excessive bail shall not be required, nor excessive fines imposed, nor cruel and unusual punishments inflicted.

Article the eleventh... The enumeration in the Constitution, of certain rights, shall not be construed to deny or disparage others retained by the people.

Article the twelfth... The powers not delegated to the United States by the Constitution, nor prohibited by it to the States, are reserved to the States respectively, or to the people.

ATTEST,

Frederick Augustus Muhlenberg, Speaker of the House of Representatives

John Adams, Vice-President of the United States, and President of the Senate

John Beckley, Clerk of the House of Representatives.

Sam. A Otis Secretary of the Senate

*Note: The capitalization and punctuation in this version is from the enrolled original of the Joint Resolution of Congress proposing the Bill of Rights, which is on permanent display in the Rotunda of the National Archives Building, Washington, D.C.*

••••••••••••••••••••••••••••••••••••••••••••••••••••••••••••••••••••••

## The Preamble to The Bill of Rights

Congress of the United States begun and held at the City of New-York, on Wednesday the fourth of March, one thousand seven hundred and eighty nine.

THE Conventions of a number of the States, having at the time of their adopting the Constitution, expressed a desire, in order to prevent misconstruction or abuse of its powers, that further declaratory and restrictive clauses should be added: And as extending the ground of public confidence in the Government, will best ensure the beneficent ends of its institution.

RESOLVED by the Senate and House of Representatives of the United States of America, in Congress assembled, two thirds of both Houses concurring, that the following Articles be proposed to the Legislatures of the several States, as amendments to the Constitution of the United States, all, or any of which Articles, when ratified by three fourths of the said Legislatures, to be valid to all intents and purposes, as part of the said Constitution; viz.

ARTICLES in addition to, and Amendment of the Constitution of the United States of America, proposed by Congress, and ratified by the Legislatures of the several States, pursuant to the fifth Article of the original Constitution.

*Note: The following text is a transcription of the first ten amendments to the Constitution in their original form. These amendments were ratified December 15, 1791, and form what is known as the "Bill of Rights." The capitalization and punctuation in this version is from the enrolled original of the Joint Resolution of Congress proposing the Bill of Rights, which is on permanent display in the Rotunda of the National Archives Building, Washington, D.C.*

.........................................................................

## The U.S. Bill of Rights

### Amendment I

Congress shall make no law respecting an establishment of religion, or prohibiting the free exercise thereof; or abridging the freedom of speech, or of the press; or the right of the people peaceably to assemble, and to petition the Government for a redress of grievances.

### Amendment II

A well regulated Militia, being necessary to the security of a free State, the right of the people to keep and bear Arms, shall not be infringed.

### Amendment III

No Soldier shall, in time of peace be quartered in any house, without the consent of the Owner, nor in time of war, but in a manner to be prescribed by law.

### Amendment IV

The right of the people to be secure in their persons, houses, papers, and effects, against unreasonable searches and seizures, shall not be violated, and no Warrants shall issue, but upon probable cause, supported by Oath or affirmation, and particularly describing the place to be searched, and the persons or things to be seized.

### Amendment V

No person shall be held to answer for a capital, or otherwise infamous crime, unless on a presentment or indictment of a Grand Jury, except in cases arising in the land or naval forces, or in the Militia, when in actual service in time of War or public danger; nor shall any person be subject for the same offence to be twice put in jeopardy of life or limb; nor shall be compelled in any criminal case to be a witness against himself, nor be deprived of life, liberty, or property, without due process of law; nor shall private property be taken for public use, without just compensation.

## Amendment VI

In all criminal prosecutions, the accused shall enjoy the right to a speedy and public trial, by an impartial jury of the State and district wherein the crime shall have been committed, which district shall have been previously ascertained by law, and to be informed of the nature and cause of the accusation; to be confronted with the witnesses against him; to have compulsory process for obtaining witnesses in his favor, and to have the Assistance of Counsel for his defence.

## Amendment VII

In Suits at common law, where the value in controversy shall exceed twenty dollars, the right of trial by jury shall be preserved, and no fact tried by a jury, shall be otherwise re-examined in any Court of the United States, than according to the rules of the common law.

## Amendment VIII

Excessive bail shall not be required, nor excessive fines imposed, nor cruel and unusual punishments inflicted.

## Amendment IX

The enumeration in the Constitution, of certain rights, shall not be construed to deny or disparage others retained by the people.

## Amendment X

The powers not delegated to the United States by the Constitution, nor prohibited by it to the States, are reserved to the States respectively, or to the people.

*Note: The Constitutional Amendments 1-10 make up what is known as The Bill of Rights. The Constitutional Amendments 11-27 are listed below.*

......................................................................................

## The Constitution: Amendments 11-27

### AMENDMENT XI
Passed by Congress March 4, 1794. Ratified February 7, 1795.

*Note: Article III, section 2, of the Constitution was modified by amendment 11.*

The Judicial power of the United States shall not be construed to extend to any suit in law or equity, commenced or prosecuted against one of the United States by Citizens of another State, or by Citizens or Subjects of any Foreign State.

### AMENDMENT XII
Passed by Congress December 9, 1803. Ratified June 15, 1804.

*Note: A portion of Article II, section 1 of the Constitution was superseded by the 12th amendment.*

The Electors shall meet in their respective states and vote by ballot for President and Vice-President, one of whom, at least, shall not be an inhabitant of the same state with themselves; they shall name in their ballots the person voted for as President, and in distinct ballots the person voted for as Vice-President, and they shall make distinct lists of all persons voted for as President, and of all persons voted for as Vice-President, and of the number of votes for each, which lists they shall sign and certify, and transmit sealed to the seat of the government of the United States, directed to the President of the Senate; - the President of the Senate shall, in the presence of the Senate and House of Representatives, open all the certificates and the votes shall then be counted; - The person having the greatest number of votes for President, shall be the President, if such number be a majority of the whole number of Electors appointed; and if no person have such majority, then from the persons having the highest numbers not exceeding three on the list of those voted for as President, the House of Representatives shall choose immediately, by ballot, the President. But in choosing the President, the votes shall be taken by states, the representation from each state having one vote; a quorum for this purpose shall consist of a member or members from two-thirds of the states, and a majority of all the states shall be necessary to a choice. [And if the House of Representatives shall not choose a President whenever the right of choice shall devolve upon them, before the fourth day of March next following, then the Vice-President shall act as President, as in case of the death or other constitutional disability of the President. - ]* The person having the greatest number of votes as Vice-President, shall be the Vice-President, if such number be a majority of the whole number of Electors appointed, and if no person have a majority, then from the two highest numbers on the list, the Senate shall choose the Vice-President; a quorum for the purpose shall consist of two-thirds of the whole number of Senators, and a majority of the whole number shall be necessary to a choice. But no person constitutionally ineligible to the office of President shall be eligible to that of Vice-President of the United States.

*Superseded by section 3 of the 20th amendment.

## AMENDMENT XIII
Passed by Congress January 31, 1865. Ratified December 6, 1865.

*Note: A portion of Article IV, section 2, of the Constitution was superseded by the 13th amendment.*

Section 1.

Neither slavery nor involuntary servitude, except as a punishment for crime whereof the party shall have been duly convicted, shall exist within the United States, or any place subject to their jurisdiction.

Section 2.

Congress shall have power to enforce this article by appropriate legislation.

## AMENDMENT XIV
Passed by Congress June 13, 1866. Ratified July 9, 1868.

*Note: Article I, section 2, of the Constitution was modified by section 2 of the 14th amendment.*

Section 1.

All persons born or naturalized in the United States, and subject to the jurisdiction thereof, are citizens of the United States and of the State wherein they reside. No State shall make or enforce any law which shall abridge the privileges or immunities of citizens of the United States; nor shall any State deprive any person of life, liberty, or property, without due process of law; nor deny to any person within its jurisdiction the equal protection of the laws.

Section 2.

Representatives shall be apportioned among the several States according to their respective numbers, counting the whole number of persons in each State, excluding Indians not taxed. But when the right to vote at any election for the choice of electors for President and Vice-President of the United States, Representatives in Congress, the Executive and Judicial officers of a State, or the members of the Legislature thereof, is denied to any of the male inhabitants of such State, being twenty-one years of age,* and citizens of the United States, or in any way abridged, except for participation in rebellion, or other crime, the basis of representation therein shall be reduced in the proportion which the number of such male citizens shall bear to the whole number of male citizens twenty-one years of age in such State.

Section 3.

No person shall be a Senator or Representative in Congress, or elector of President and Vice-President, or hold any office, civil or military, under the United States, or under any State, who, having previously taken an oath, as a member of Congress, or as an officer of the United States, or as a member of any State legislature, or as an executive or judicial officer of any State, to support the Constitution of the United States, shall have engaged in insurrection or rebellion against the same, or given aid or comfort to the enemies thereof. But Congress may by a vote of two-thirds of each House, remove such disability.

Section 4.

The validity of the public debt of the United States, authorized by law, including debts incurred for payment of pensions and bounties for services in suppressing insurrection or rebellion, shall not be questioned. But neither the United States nor any State shall assume or pay any debt or obligation incurred in aid of insurrection or rebellion against the United States, or any claim for the loss or emancipation of any slave; but all such debts, obligations and claims shall be held illegal and void.

Section 5.

The Congress shall have the power to enforce, by appropriate legislation, the provisions of this article.

*Changed by section 1 of the 26th amendment.*

## AMENDMENT XV
Passed by Congress February 26, 1869. Ratified February 3, 1870.

Section 1.

The right of citizens of the United States to vote shall not be denied or abridged by the United States or by any State on account of race, color, or previous condition of servitude.

Section 2.

The Congress shall have the power to enforce this article by appropriate legislation.

## AMENDMENT XVI
Passed by Congress July 2, 1909. Ratified February 3, 1913.

*Note: Article I, section 9, of the Constitution was modified by amendment 16.*

The Congress shall have power to lay and collect taxes on incomes, from whatever source derived, without apportionment among the several States, and without regard to any census or enumeration.

## AMENDMENT XVII
Passed by Congress May 13, 1912. Ratified April 8, 1913.

*Note: Article I, section 3, of the Constitution was modified by the 17th amendment.*

The Senate of the United States shall be composed of two Senators from each State, elected by the people thereof, for six years; and each Senator shall have one vote. The electors in each State shall have the qualifications requisite for electors of the most numerous branch of the State legislatures.

When vacancies happen in the representation of any State in the Senate, the executive authority of such State shall issue writs of election to fill such vacancies: Provided, That the legislature of any State may empower the executive thereof to make temporary appointments until the people fill the vacancies by election as the legislature may direct.

This amendment shall not be so construed as to affect the election or term of any Senator chosen before it becomes valid as part of the Constitution.

## AMENDMENT XVIII
Passed by Congress December 18, 1917. Ratified January 16, 1919. Repealed by Amendment 21.

Section 1.

After one year from the ratification of this article the manufacture, sale, or transportation of intoxicating liquors within, the importation thereof into, or the exportation thereof from the United States and all territory subject to the jurisdiction thereof for beverage purposes is hereby prohibited.

Section 2.

The Congress and the several States shall have concurrent power to enforce this article by appropriate legislation.

Section 3.

This article shall be inoperative unless it shall have been ratified as an amendment to the Constitution by the legislatures of the several States, as provided in the Constitution, within seven years from the date of the submission hereof to the States by the Congress.

## AMENDMENT XIX
Passed by Congress June 4, 1919. Ratified August 18, 1920.

The right of citizens of the United States to vote shall not be denied or abridged by the United States or by any State on account of sex.

Congress shall have power to enforce this article by appropriate legislation.

## AMENDMENT XX
Passed by Congress March 2, 1932. Ratified January 23, 1933.

*Note: Article I, section 4, of the Constitution was modified by section 2 of this amendment. In addition, a portion of the 12th amendment was superseded by section 3.*

Section 1.

The terms of the President and the Vice President shall end at noon on the 20th day of January, and the terms of Senators and Representatives at noon on the 3d day of January, of the years in which such terms would have ended if this article had not been ratified; and the terms of their successors shall then begin.

Section 2.

The Congress shall assemble at least once in every year, and such meeting shall begin at noon on the 3d day of January, unless they shall by law appoint a different day.

Section 3.

If, at the time fixed for the beginning of the term of the President, the President elect shall have died, the Vice President elect shall become President. If a President shall not have been chosen before the time fixed for the beginning of his term, or if the President elect shall have failed to qualify, then the Vice President elect shall act as President until a President shall have qualified; and the Congress may by law provide for the case wherein neither a President elect nor a Vice President elect shall have qualified, declaring who shall then act as President, or the manner in which one who is to act shall be selected, and such person shall act accordingly until a President or Vice President shall have qualified.

Section 4.

The Congress may by law provide for the case of the death of any of the persons from whom the House of Representatives may choose a President whenever the right of choice shall have devolved upon them, and for the case of the death of any of the persons from whom the Senate may choose a Vice President whenever the right of choice shall have devolved upon them.

Section 5.

Sections 1 and 2 shall take effect on the 15th day of October following the ratification of this article.

Section 6.

This article shall be inoperative unless it shall have been ratified as an amendment to the Constitution by the legislatures of three-fourths of the several States within seven years from the date of its submission.

## AMENDMENT XXI
Passed by Congress February 20, 1933. Ratified December 5, 1933.

Section 1.

The eighteenth article of amendment to the Constitution of the United States is hereby repealed.

Section 2.

The transportation or importation into any State, Territory, or possession of the United States for delivery or use therein of intoxicating liquors, in violation of the laws thereof, is hereby prohibited.

Section 3.

This article shall be inoperative unless it shall have been ratified as an amendment to the Constitution by conventions in the several States, as provided in the Constitution, within seven years from the date of the submission hereof to the States by the Congress.

## AMENDMENT XXII
Passed by Congress March 21, 1947. Ratified February 27, 1951.

Section 1.

No person shall be elected to the office of the President more than twice, and no person who has held the office of President, or acted as President, for more than two years of a term to which some other person was elected President shall be elected to the office of the President more than once. But this Article shall not apply to any person holding the office of President when this Article was proposed by the Congress, and shall not prevent any person who may be holding the office of President, or acting as President, during the term within which this Article becomes operative from holding the office of President or acting as President during the remainder of such term.

Section 2.

This article shall be inoperative unless it shall have been ratified as an amendment to the Constitution by the legislatures of three-fourths of the several States within seven years from the date of its submission to the States by the Congress.

## AMENDMENT XXIII
Passed by Congress June 16, 1960. Ratified March 29, 1961.

Section 1.

The District constituting the seat of Government of the United States shall appoint in such manner as the Congress may direct:

A number of electors of President and Vice President equal to the whole number of Senators and Representatives in Congress to which the District would be entitled if it were a State, but in no event more than the least populous State; they shall be in addition to those appointed by the States, but they shall be considered, for the purposes of the election of President and Vice President, to be electors appointed by a State; and they shall meet in the District and perform such duties as provided by the twelfth article of amendment.

Section 2.

The Congress shall have power to enforce this article by appropriate legislation.

## AMENDMENT XXIV
Passed by Congress August 27, 1962. Ratified January 23, 1964.

Section 1.

The right of citizens of the United States to vote in any primary or other election for President or Vice President, for electors for President or Vice President, or for Senator or Representative in Congress, shall not be denied or abridged by the United States or any State by reason of failure to pay any poll tax or other tax.

Section 2.

The Congress shall have power to enforce this article by appropriate legislation.

**AMENDMENT XXV**
Passed by Congress July 6, 1965. Ratified February 10, 1967.

Note: Article II, section 1, of the Constitution was affected by the 25th amendment.

Section 1.

In case of the removal of the President from office or of his death or resignation, the Vice President shall become President.

Section 2.

Whenever there is a vacancy in the office of the Vice President, the President shall nominate a Vice President who shall take office upon confirmation by a majority vote of both Houses of Congress.

Section 3.

Whenever the President transmits to the President pro tempore of the Senate and the Speaker of the House of Representatives his written declaration that he is unable to discharge the powers and duties of his office, and until he transmits to them a written declaration to the contrary, such powers and duties shall be discharged by the Vice President as Acting President.

Section 4.

Whenever the Vice President and a majority of either the principal officers of the executive departments or of such other body as Congress may by law provide, transmit to the President pro tempore of the Senate and the Speaker of the House of Representatives their written declaration that the President is unable to discharge the powers and duties of his office, the Vice President shall immediately assume the powers and duties of the office as Acting President.

Thereafter, when the President transmits to the President pro tempore of the Senate and the Speaker of the House of Representatives his written declaration that no inability exists, he shall resume the powers and duties of his office unless the Vice President and a majority of either the principal officers of the executive department or of such other body as Congress may by law provide, transmit within four days to the President pro tempore of the Senate and the Speaker of the House of Representatives their written declaration that the President is unable to discharge the powers and duties of his office. Thereupon Congress shall decide the issue, assembling within forty-eight hours for that purpose if not in session. If the Congress, within twenty-one days after receipt of the latter written declaration, or, if Congress is not in session, within twenty-one days after Congress is required to assemble, determines by two-thirds vote of both Houses that the President is unable to discharge the powers and duties of his office, the Vice President shall continue to discharge the same as Acting President; otherwise, the President shall resume the powers and duties of his office.

## AMENDMENT XXVI
Passed by Congress March 23, 1971. Ratified July 1, 1971.

Note: Amendment 14, section 2, of the Constitution was modified by section 1 of the 26th amendment.

Section 1.

The right of citizens of the United States, who are eighteen years of age or older, to vote shall not be denied or abridged by the United States or by any State on account of age.

Section 2.

The Congress shall have power to enforce this article by appropriate legislation.

## AMENDMENT XXVII
Originally proposed Sept. 25, 1789. Ratified May 7, 1992.

No law, varying the compensation for the services of the Senators and Representatives, shall take effect, until an election of Representatives shall have intervened.

## The Founding Fathers: Connecticut

### Oliver Ellsworth, Connecticut

Oliver Ellsworth was born on April 29, 1745, in Windsor, CT, to Capt. David and Jemima Ellsworth. Oliver entered Yale in 1762 but transferred to the College of New Jersey (later Princeton) at the end of his second year. He continued to study theology and received his A.B. degree after two years. Soon afterward, however, Ellsworth turned to the law. After four years of study, he was admitted to the bar in 1771. The next year Ellsworth married Abigail Wolcott.

Despite a slow start, Ellsworth built up a prosperous law practice. His reputation as an able and industrious jurist grew, and in 1777 Ellsworth became Connecticut's state attorney for Hartford County. That same year he was chosen as one of Connecticut's representatives in the Continental Congress. He served on various committees during six annual terms until 1783. Ellsworth was also active in his state's efforts during the Revolution. As a member of the Committee of the Pay Table, Oliver Ellsworth was one of the five men who supervised Connecticut's war expenditures. In 1779 he assumed greater duties as a member of the council of safety, which, with the governor, controlled all military measures for the state.

When the Constitutional Convention met in Philadelphia in 1787, Ellsworth once again represented Connecticut and took an active part in the proceedings. During debate on the Great Compromise, Ellsworth proposed that the basis of representation in the legislative branch remain by state, as under the Articles of Confederation. He also left his mark through an amendment to change the word "national" to "United States" in a resolution. Thereafter, "United States" was the title used in the convention to designate the government.

Ellsworth also served on the Committee of Five that prepared the first draft of the Constitution. Ellsworth favored the three-fifths compromise on the enumeration of slaves but opposed the abolition of the foreign slave trade. Though he left the convention near the end of August and did not sign the final document, he urged its adoption upon his return to Connecticut and wrote the Letters of a Landholder to promote its ratification.

Ellsworth served as one of Connecticut's first two senators in the new federal government between 1789 and 1796. In the Senate he chaired the committee that framed the bill organizing the federal judiciary and helped to work out the practical details necessary to run a new government. Ellsworth's other achievements in Congress included framing the measure that admitted North Carolina to the Union, devising the non-intercourse act that forced Rhode Island to join, drawing up the bill to regulate the consular service, and serving on the committee that considered Alexander Hamilton's plan for funding the national debt and for incorporating the Bank of the United States.

In the spring of 1796 he was appointed Chief Justice of the Supreme Court and also served as commissioner to France in 1799 and 1800. Upon his return to America in early 1801, Ellsworth retired from public life and lived in Windsor, CT. He died there on November 26, 1807, and was buried in the cemetery of the First Church of Windsor.

## William Samuel Johnson, Connecticut

William Samuel Johnson was the son of Samuel Johnson, the first president of King's College (later Columbia College and University). William was born at Stratford, CT, in 1727. His father, who was a well-known Anglican clergyman-philosopher, prepared him for college and he graduated from Yale in 1744. About three years later he won a master of arts degree from the same institution and an honorary master's from Harvard.

Resisting his father's wish that he become a minister, Johnson embraced law instead - largely by educating himself and without benefit of formal training. After admittance to the bar, he launched a practice in Stratford, representing clients from nearby New York State as well as Connecticut, and before long he established business connections with various mercantile houses in New York City. In 1749, adding to his already substantial wealth, he married Anne Beach, daughter of a local businessman. The couple was to have five daughters and six sons, but many of them died at an early age.

Johnson did not shirk the civic responsibilities of one of his station. In the 1750s he began his public career as a Connecticut militia officer. In 1761 and 1765 he served in the lower house of the colonial assembly. In 1766 and 1771 he was elected to the upper house. At the time of the Revolution, Johnson was disturbed by conflicting loyalties. Although he attended the Stamp Act Congress in 1765, moderately opposed the Townshend Duties of 1767, and believed that most British policies were unwise, he retained strong transatlantic ties and found it difficult to choose sides. Many of his friends resided in Britain; in 1765 and 1766 Oxford University conferred honorary master's and doctor's degrees upon him; he had a strong association with the Anglican Church; he acted as Connecticut's agent in Britain during the years 1767-71; and he was friendly with men such as Jared Ingersoll, Sr., who were affiliated with the British administration.

Johnson finally decided to work for peace between Britain and the colonies and to oppose the extremist Whig faction. On that basis, he refused to participate in the First Continental Congress, to which he was elected in 1774, following service as a judge of the Connecticut colonial supreme court (1772-74). When hostilities broke out, he confined his activities to peacemaking efforts. In April 1775 Connecticut sent him and another emissary to speak to British Gen. Thomas Gage about ending the bloodshed. But the time was not ripe for negotiations and they failed. Johnson fell out of favor with radical patriot elements who gained the ascendancy in Connecticut government and they no longer called upon his service. Although he was arrested in 1779 on charges of communicating with the enemy, he cleared himself and was released.

Once the passions of war had ebbed, Johnson resumed his political career. In the Continental Congress (1785-87), he was one of the most influential and popular delegates. Playing a major role in the Constitutional Convention, he missed no sessions after arriving on June 2; espoused the Connecticut Compromise; and chaired the Committee of Style, which shaped the final document. He also worked for ratification in Connecticut.

Johnson took part in the new government, in the U.S. Senate where he contributed to passage of the Judiciary Act of 1789. In 1791, the year after the government moved from New York to Philadelphia, he resigned mainly because he preferred to devote all his energies to the presidency of Columbia College (1787-1800), in New York City. During these years, he established the school on a firm basis and recruited a fine faculty.

Johnson retired from the college in 1800, a few years after his wife died, and in the same year wed Mary Brewster Beach, a relative of his first bride. They resided at his birthplace, Stratford. He died there in 1819 at the age of 92 and was buried at Old Episcopal Cemetery.

## Roger Sherman, Connecticut

In 1723, when Sherman was two years of age, his family relocated from his Newton, MA, birthplace to Dorchester (present Stoughton). As a boy, he was spurred by a desire to learn and read widely in his spare time to supplement his minimal education at a common school. But he spent most of his waking hours helping his father with farming chores and learning the cobbler's trade from him. In 1743, two years after his father's death, Sherman joined an elder brother who had settled in New Milford, CT.

Purchasing a store, becoming a county surveyor, and winning a variety of town offices, Sherman prospered and assumed leadership in the community. In 1749 he married Elizabeth Hartwell, by whom he had seven children. Without benefit of a formal legal education, he was admitted to the bar in 1754 and embarked upon a distinguished judicial and political career. In the period 1755-61, except for a brief interval, he served as a representative in the colonial legislature and held the offices of justice of the peace and county judge. Somehow he also eked out time to publish an essay on monetary theory and a series of almanacs incorporating his own astronomical observations and verse.

In 1761, Sherman abandoned his law practice, and moved to New Haven, CT. There, he managed two stores, one that catered to Yale students, and another in nearby Wallingford. He also became a friend and benefactor of Yale College, and served for many years as its treasurer. In 1763, or three years after the death of his first wife, he wed Rebecca Prescott, who bore eight children.

Meanwhile, Sherman's political career had blossomed. He rose from justice of the peace and county judge to an associate judge of the Connecticut Superior Court and to representative in both houses of the colonial assembly. Although opposed to extremism, he promptly joined the fight against Britain. He supported nonimportation measures and headed the New Haven committee of correspondence.

Sherman was a longtime and influential member of the Continental Congress (1774-81 and 1783-84). He won membership on the committees that drafted the Declaration of Independence and the Articles of Confederation, as well as those concerned with Indian affairs, national finances, and military matters. To solve economic problems, at both national and state levels, he advocated high taxes rather than excessive borrowing or the issuance of paper currency.

While in Congress, Sherman remained active in state and local politics, continuing to hold the office of judge of the Connecticut Superior Court, as well as membership on the council of safety (1777-79). In 1783 he helped codify Connecticut's statutory laws. The next year, he was elected mayor of New Haven (1784-86).

Although on the edge of insolvency, mainly because of wartime losses, Sherman could not resist the lure of national service. In 1787 he represented his state at the Constitutional Convention, and attended practically every session. Not only did he sit on the Committee on Postponed Matters, but he also probably helped draft the New Jersey Plan and was a prime mover behind the Connecticut, or Great, Compromise, which broke the deadlock between the large and small states over representation. He was, in addition, instrumental in Connecticut's ratification of the Constitution.

Sherman concluded his career by serving in the U.S. House of Representatives (1789-91) and Senate (1791-93), where he espoused the Federalist cause. He died at New Haven in 1793 at the age of 72 and is buried in the Grove Street Cemetery.

## The Founding Fathers: Delaware

### Richard Bassett, Delaware

Bassett (Basset) was born in Cecil County, MD., in April 1745. After his tavern-keeper father deserted his mother, he was reared by a relative, Peter Lawson, from whom he later inherited Bohemia Manor (MD.) estate. He read for the law at Philadelphia and in 1770 received a license to practice in Dover, DE. He prospered as a lawyer and planter, and eventually came to own not only Bohemia Manor, but homes in Dover and Wilmington as well.

During the Revolution, Bassett captained a troop of Dover cavalry militia and served on the Delaware council of safety. Subsequently, he participated in Delaware's constitutional convention and sat in both the upper and lower houses of the legislature. In 1786 he represented his state in the Annapolis Convention.

At the U.S. Constitutional Convention the next year, Bassett attended diligently but made no speeches, served on no committees, and cast no critical votes. Like several other delegates of estimable reputation and talent, he allowed others to make the major steps.

Bassett subsequently went on to a bright career in the state and federal governments. In the Delaware ratifying convention, he joined in the 30-0 vote for the Constitution. Subsequently, in the years 1789-93, he served in the U.S. Senate. In that capacity, he voted in favor of the power of the President to remove governmental officers and against Hamilton's plan for the federal assumption of state debts.

From 1793 until 1799 Bassett held the chief justiceship of the court of common pleas. He espoused the Federalist cause in the 1790s, and served as a Presidential elector on behalf of John Adams in 1797. Two years later, Bassett was elected Governor of Delaware and continued in that post until 1801. That year, he became one of President Adams' "midnight" appointments as a judge of the U.S. Circuit Court. Subsequently, the Jeffersonian Republicans abolished his judgeship, and he spent the rest of his life in retirement.

Twice married, to Ann Ennals and a woman named Bruff, Bassett fathered several children. He was a devout Methodist, held religious meetings at Bohemia Manor, and supported the church financially. He died in 1815 at the age of 70 and is interred at the Wilmington and Brandywine Cemetery, Wilmington, DE.

### Gunning Bedford, Jr., Delaware

Bedford was born in 1747 at Philadelphia and reared there. The fifth of seven children, he was descended from a distinguished family that originally settled in Jamestown, VA. He usually referred to himself as Gunning Bedford, Jr., to avoid confusion with his cousin and contemporary Delaware statesman and soldier, Col. Gunning Bedford.

In 1771 signer Bedford graduated with honors from the College of New Jersey (later Princeton), where he was a classmate of James Madison. Apparently while still in school, Bedford wed Jane B. Parker, who bore at least one daughter. After reading law with Joseph Read in Philadelphia, Bedford won admittance to the bar and set up a practice. Subsequently, he moved to Dover and then to Wilmington. He apparently served in the Continental Army, possibly as an aide to General Washington.

Following the war, Bedford figured prominently in the politics of his state and nation. He sat in the legislature, on the state council, and in the Continental Congress (1783-85). In the latter year, he was chosen as a delegate to the Annapolis Convention but for some reason did not attend. From 1784 to 1789 he was attorney general of Delaware.

Bedford numbered among the more active members of the Constitutional Convention, and he missed few sessions. A large and forceful man, he spoke on several occasions and was a member of the committee that drafted the Great Compromise. An ardent small-state advocate, he attacked the pretensions of the large states over the small and warned that the latter might be forced to seek foreign alliances unless their interests were accommodated. He attended the Delaware ratifying convention.

For another two years, Bedford continued as Delaware's attorney general. In 1789 Washington designated him as a federal district judge for his state, an office he was to occupy for the rest of his life. His only other ventures into national politics came in 1789 and 1793, as a Federalist presidential elector. In the main, however, he spent his later years in judicial pursuits, in aiding Wilmington Academy, in fostering abolitionism, and in enjoying his Lombardy Hall farm.

Bedford died at the age of 65 in 1812 and was buried in the First Presbyterian Churchyard in Wilmington. Later, when the cemetery was abandoned, his body was transferred to the Masonic Home, on the Lancaster Turnpike in Christiana Hundred, DE.

## Jacob Broom, Delaware

Broom was born in 1752 at Wilmington, DE., the eldest son of a blacksmith who prospered in farming. The youth was educated at home and probably at the local Old Academy. Although he followed his father into farming and also studied surveying, he was to make his career primarily in mercantile pursuits, including shipping and the import trade, and in real estate. In 1773 he married Rachel Pierce, who bore eight children.

Broom was not a distinguished patriot. His only recorded service was the preparation of maps for George Washington before the Battle of Brandywine, PA. In 1776, at 24 years of age, Broom became assistant burgess of Wilmington. Over the next several decades, he held that office six times and that of chief burgess four times, as well as those of borough assessor, president of the city "street regulators," and justice of the peace for New Castle County.

Broom sat in the state legislature in the years 1784-86 and 1788, during which time he was chosen as a delegate to the Annapolis Convention, but he did not attend. At the Constitutional Convention, he never missed a session and spoke on several occasions, but his role was only a minor one.

After the convention, Broom returned to Wilmington, where in 1795 he erected a home near the Brandywine River on the outskirts of the city. He was its first postmaster (1790-92) and continued to hold various local offices and to participate in a variety of economic endeavors. For many years, he chaired the board of directors of Wilmington's Delaware Bank. He also operated a cotton mill, as well as a machine shop that produced and repaired mill machinery. He was involved, too, in an unsuccessful scheme to mine bog iron ore. A further interest was internal improvements: toll roads, canals, and bridges.

Broom also found time for philanthropic and religious activities. He served on the board of trustees of the College of Wilmington and as a lay leader at Old Swedes Church. He died at the age of 58 in 1810 while in Philadelphia on business and was buried there at Christ Church Burial Ground.

## John Dickinson, Delaware

Dickinson, "Penman of the Revolution," was born in 1732 at Crosiadore estate, near the village of Trappe in Talbot County, Maryland. He was the first son of Samuel Dickinson, the prosperous farmer, and his second wife, Mary (Cadwalader) Dickinson. In 1740, the family moved to Kent County near Dover, Delaware, where private tutors educated the youth. In 1750, he began to study law with John Moland in Philadelphia. In 1753, Dickinson went to England to continue his studies at London's Middle Temple. Four years later, he returned to Philadelphia and became a prominent lawyer there. In 1770, he married Mary Norris, daughter of a wealthy merchant. The couple had two daughters.

By that time, Dickinson's superior education and talents had propelled him into politics. In 1760, he had served in the assembly of the Three Lower Counties (Delaware), where he held the speakership. Combining his Pennsylvania and Delaware careers in 1762, he won a seat as a Philadelphia member in the Pennsylvania assembly where he remained through 1765. He became the leader of the conservative side in the colony's political battles. His defense of the Quaker charter against the faction led by Benjamin Franklin earned him respect for his integrity and Franklin lost his seat in the assembly.

In the meantime, the struggle between the colonies and the mother country had waxed strong and Dickinson had emerged in the forefront of Revolutionary thinkers. In the debates over the Stamp Act (1765), he played a key part serving as de facto leader of the Stamp Act Congress and authoring its publications. Later that year, he wrote The Late Regulations Respecting the British Colonies… Considered, an influential pamphlet that urged Americans to seek repeal of the act by pressuring British merchants.

In 1767-68, in response to the Townshend Duties, Dickinson wrote a series of newspaper articles entitled "Letters from a Farmer in Pennsylvania." They attacked British taxation policy and urged resistance to unjust laws, but also emphasized the possibility of a peaceful resolution. So popular were the "Letters" in the colonies that Dickinson received an honorary LL.D. from the College of New Jersey (later Princeton), public thanks from a meeting in Boston, accolades from around the colonies, and international celebrity. He championed rigorous colonial resistance in the form of nonimportation and nonexportation agreements and peaceful means of resistance, including civil disobedience.

In 1771, Dickinson returned to the Pennsylvania legislature and drafted a petition to the king that was unanimously approved. He particularly resented the tactics of New England leaders in that year and refused to support aid requested by Boston in the wake of the Intolerable Acts, though he sympathized with the city's plight. In 1774 he chaired the Philadelphia committee of correspondence and briefly sat in the First Continental Congress as a representative from Pennsylvania. He authored four of the six documents published by Congress.

Throughout 1775, Dickinson supported American rights and liberties, but continued to work for peace. He drew up petitions asking the king for redress of grievances. At the same time, he chaired a Philadelphia committee of safety and defense and held a colonelcy in the first battalion recruited in Philadelphia to defend the city.

After Lexington and Concord, Dickinson continued to hope for a peaceful solution. In the Second Continental Congress (1775-76), still a representative of Pennsylvania, he drew up the Olive Branch Petition and the "Declaration of the Causes of Taking Up Arms." In the Pennsylvania assembly in November 1775, he drafted instructions to the delegates to Congress directing them to seek redress of grievances, but ordered them to oppose separation of the colonies from Britain. In June 1776, he wrote new instructions allowing them to vote for independence, but not expressly instructing them to do so.

By that time, Dickinson's moderate position had left him in the minority, but he nevertheless was asked to draft the Articles of Confederation. In Congress, he abstained from the vote on the Declaration of Independence (1776) and refused to sign it. Nevertheless, he then became one of only two contemporary congressional members (with Thomas McKean) who entered the military. During the summer, while on the New Jersey front, he was voted out of the Pennsylvania assembly. When much of his unit deserted, he resigned his colonelcy and accepted reelection to the Pennsylvania assembly in the fall of 1776. When the revolutionary government would not consider amending the new constitution to protect dissenters' rights, he resigned his seat. He then enlisted as a private in the Delaware militia and may have taken part in the Battle of Brandywine, Pennsylvania (September 11, 1777). He was given a commission as brigadier general in the Delaware militia, but he appears not to have acted on it.

Dickinson took a seat in the Continental Congress (1779), where he signed the Articles of Confederation, although a much different version from the one he had drafted. In 1781, he became president of Delaware's Supreme Executive Council. Before his tenure was over, he was elected president of Pennsylvania (1782-85). In 1786, representing Delaware, he attended and chaired the Annapolis Convention and authored the letter to Congress calling for the Constitutional Convention.

The next year, Delaware sent Dickinson to the Constitutional Convention. He missed a number of sessions and left early because of illness, but he made worthwhile contributions, including engineering the solution for representation known as the Connecticut Compromise and arguing for the end of the slave trade. Because of his premature departure from the convention, he did not actually sign the Constitution but authorized his friend and fellow-delegate George Read to do so for him. From home he wrote the Fabius Letters (1788) arguing for ratification.

Dickinson continued to be active in public affairs. In 1792 he served as president of the Delaware Constitutional Convention, in 1795 he led citizen opposition to the Jay Treaty, and he served as informal advisor to politicians, including Senator George Logan, Attorney General Caesar A. Rodney, and President Thomas Jefferson. In addition to continuing to publish pamphlets on current events, in 1801 he published two volumes of his collected works. He died at Wilmington in 1808 at the age of 75 and was entombed in the Friends Burial Ground.

## George Read, Delaware

Read's mother was the daughter of a Welsh planter, and his Dublin-born father a landholder of means. Soon after George's birth in 1733 near the village of North East in Cecil County, MD, his family moved to New Castle, DE, where the youth, who was one of six sons, grew up. He attended school at Chester, PA, and Rev. Francis Alison's academy at New London, PA, and about the age of 15 he began reading with a Philadelphia lawyer.

In 1753 Read was admitted to the bar and began to practice. The next year, he journeyed back to New Castle, hung out his shingle, and before long enlisted a clientele that extended into Maryland. During this period he resided in New Castle but maintained Stonum a country retreat near the city. In 1763 he wed Gertrude Ross Till, the widowed sister of George Ross, like Read a future signer of the Declaration of Independence. She bore four sons and a daughter.

While crown attorney general (1763-74) for the Three Lower Counties (present Delaware), Read protested against the Stamp Act. In 1765 he began a career in the colonial legislature that lasted more than a decade. A moderate Whig, he supported nonimportation measures and dignified protests. His attendance at the Continental Congress (1774-77) was irregular. Like his friend John Dickinson, he was willing to protect colonial rights but was wary of extremism. He voted against independence on July 2, 1776, the only signer of the Declaration to do so, apparently either bowing to the strong Tory sentiment in Delaware, or believing reconciliation with Britain was still possible.

That same year, Read gave priority to state responsibilities. He presided over the Delaware constitutional convention, in which he chaired the drafting committee, and began a term as speaker of the legislative council, which in effect made him vice president of the state. When the British took Wilmington the next fall, they captured the president, a resident of the city.

At first, because Read was away in Congress, Thomas McKean, speaker of the lower house, took over as acting president. But in November, after barely escaping from the British himself while he and his family were en route to Dover from Philadelphia, newly occupied by the redcoats, Read assumed the office and held it until the spring of 1778. Back in the legislative council, in 1779 he drafted the act directing Delaware congressional delegates to sign the Articles of Confederation.

During 1779, in poor health, Read resigned from the legislative council, refused reelection to Congress, and began a period of inactivity. During the years 1782-88, he again sat on the council and concurrently held the position of judge of the court of appeals in admiralty cases.

Meantime, in 1784, Read had served on a commission that adjusted New York-Massachusetts land claims. In 1786 he attended the Annapolis Convention. The next year, he participated in the Constitutional Convention, where he missed few if any sessions and championed the rights of the small states. Otherwise, he adopted a Hamiltonian stance, favoring a strong executive. He later led the ratification movement in Delaware, the first state to ratify.

In the U.S. Senate (1789-93), Read's attendance was again erratic, but when present he allied with the Federalists. He resigned to accept the post of chief justice of Delaware. He held it until his death at New Castle five years later, just three days after he celebrated his 65th birthday. His grave is there in the Immanuel Episcopal Churchyard.

## The Founding Fathers: Georgia

### Abraham Baldwin, Georgia

Baldwin was born in Guilford, Conn., in 1754, the second son of a blacksmith who fathered 12 children by two wives. Besides Abraham, several of the family attained distinction. His sister Ruth married the poet and diplomat Joel Barlow, and his half-brother Henry attained the position of justice of the U.S. Supreme Court. Their ambitious father went heavily into debt to educate his children.

After attending a local village school, Abraham matriculated at Yale, in nearby New Haven. He graduated in 1772. Three years later, he became a minister and tutor at the college. He held that position until 1779, when he served as a chaplain in the Continental Army. Two years later, he declined an offer from his alma mater of a professorship of divinity. Instead of resuming his ministerial or educational duties after the war, he turned to the study of law and in 1783 gained admittance to the bar at Fairfield, CT.

Within a year, Baldwin moved to Georgia, won legislative approval to practice his profession, and obtained a grant of land in Wilkes County. In 1785 he sat in the assembly and the Continental Congress. Two years later, his father died and Baldwin undertook to pay off his debts and educate, out of his own pocket, his half-brothers and half-sisters.

That same year, Baldwin attended the Constitutional Convention, from which he was absent for a few weeks. Although usually inconspicuous, he sat on the Committee on Postponed Matters and helped resolve the large-small state representation crisis. At first, he favored representation in the Senate based upon property holdings, but possibly because of his close relationship with the Connecticut delegation he later came to fear alienation of the small states and changed his mind to representation by state.

After the convention, Baldwin returned to the Continental Congress (1787-89). He was then elected to the U.S. Congress, where he served for 18 years (House of Representatives, 1789-99; Senate, 1799-1807). During these years, he became a bitter opponent of Hamiltonian policies and, unlike most other native New Englanders, an ally of Madison and Jefferson and the Democratic-Republicans. In the Senate, he presided for a while as president pro tem.

By 1790 Baldwin had taken up residence in Augusta. Beginning in the preceding decade, he had begun efforts to advance the educational system in Georgia. Appointed with six others in 1784 to oversee the founding of a state college, he saw his dream come true in 1798 when Franklin College was founded. Modeled after Yale, it became the nucleus of the University of Georgia.

Baldwin, who never married, died after a short illness during his 53d year in 1807. Still serving in the Senate at the time, he was buried in Washington's Rock Creek Cemetery.

## William Few, Georgia

Few was born in 1748. His father's family had emigrated from England to Pennsylvania in the 1680s, but the father had subsequently moved to Maryland, where he married and settled on a farm near Baltimore. William was born there. He encountered much hardship and received minimal schooling. When he was 10 years of age, his father, seeking better opportunity, moved his family to North Carolina.

In 1771 Few, his father, and a brother associated themselves with the "Regulators," a group of frontiersmen who opposed the royal governor. As a result, the brother was hanged, the Few family farm was destroyed, and the father was forced to move once again, this time to Georgia. William remained behind, helping to settle his father's affairs, until 1776 when he joined his family near Wrightsboro, Ga. About this time, he won admittance to the bar, based on earlier informal study, and set up practice in Augusta.

When the War for Independence began, Few enthusiastically aligned himself with the Whig cause. Although largely self-educated, he soon proved his capacity for leadership and won a lieutenant-colonelcy in the dragoons. In addition, he entered politics. He was elected to the Georgia provincial congress of 1776 and during the war twice served in the assembly, in 1777 and 1779. During the same period, he also sat on the state executive council besides holding the positions of surveyor-general and Indian commissioner. He also served in the Continental Congress (1780-88), during which time he was reelected to the Georgia Assembly (1783).

Four years later, Few was appointed as one of six state delegates to the Constitutional Convention, two of whom never attended and two others of whom did not stay for the duration. Few himself missed large segments of the proceedings, being absent during all of July and part of August because of congressional service, and never made a speech. Nonetheless, he contributed nationalist votes at critical times. Furthermore, as a delegate to the last sessions of the Continental Congress, he helped steer the Constitution past its first obstacle, approval by Congress. And he attended the state ratifying convention.

Few became one of his state's first U.S. senators (1789-93). When his term ended, he headed back home and served again in the assembly. In 1796 he received an appointment as a federal judge for the Georgia circuit. For reasons unknown, he resigned his judgeship in 1799 at the age of 52 and moved to New York City.

Few's career continued to blossom. He served four years in the legislature (1802-5) and then as inspector of prisons (1802-10), alderman (1813-14), and U.S. commissioner of loans (1804). From 1804 to 1814 he held a directorship at the Manhattan Bank and later the presidency of City Bank. A devout Methodist, he also donated generously to philanthropic causes.

When Few died in 1828 at the age of 80 in Fishkill-on-the-Hudson (present Beacon), he was survived by his wife (born Catherine Nicholson) and three daughters. Originally buried in the yard of the local Reformed Dutch Church, his body was later reinterred at St. Paul's Church, Augusta, GA.

## William Houston, Georgia

William Houston was the son of Sir Patrick Houston, a member of the council under the royal government of Georgia. He was born in 1755 in Savannah, GA. Houston received a liberal education, which included legal training at Inner Temple in London. The War for Independence cut short his training, and Houston returned home to Georgia. For many years members of Houston's family had been high officials in the colony. With the onset of war, many remained loyal to the crown, but William, a zealous advocate of colonists' rights, was among the first to counsel resistance to British aggression.

Houston represented Georgia in the Continental Congress from 1783 through 1786. He was chosen as one of Georgia's agents to settle a boundary dispute with South Carolina in 1785 and was one of the original trustees of the University of Georgia at Athens.

When the Constitutional Convention convened in 1787, Houston presented his credentials as one of Georgia's delegates. He stayed for only a short time, from June 1 until about July 23, but he was present during the debate on the representation question. Houston split Georgia's vote on equal representation in the Senate, voting "nay" against Abraham Baldwin's "aye."

Houston died in Savannah on March 17, 1813, and was interred in St. Paul's Chapel, New York City.

## William Leigh Pierce, Georgia

Very little is known about William Pierce's early life. He was probably born in Georgia in 1740, but he grew up in Virginia. During the Revolutionary War Pierce acted as an aide-de-camp to Gen. Nathanael Greene and eventually attained the rank of brevet major. For his conduct at the battle of Eutaw Springs, Congress presented him with a ceremonial sword.

The year Pierce left the army, 1783, he married Charlotte Fenwick of South Carolina. They had two sons, one of whom died as a child. Pierce made his home in Savannah, where he engaged in business. He first organized an import-export company, Pierce, White, and Call, in 1783, but it dissolved less than a year later. He made a new start with his wife's dowry and formed William Pierce & Company. In 1786 he was a member of the Georgia House of Representatives and was also elected to the Continental Congress.

At the Constitutional Convention Pierce did not play a large role, but he exerted some influence and participated in three debates. He argued for the election of one house of the federal legislature by the people and one house by the states; he favored a 3-year term instead of a 7-year term in the second house. Because he agreed that the Articles had been insufficient, he recommended strengthening the federal government at the expense of state privileges as long as state distinctions were not altogether destroyed. Pierce approved of the resulting Constitution, but he found it necessary to leave in the middle of the proceedings. A decline in the European rice market adversely affected his business. Soon after he returned to Savannah he went bankrupt, having "neither the skill of an experienced merchant nor any reserve capital." Only two years later, on December 10, 1789, Pierce died in Savannah at age 49 leaving tremendous debts.

Pierce's notes on the proceedings of the convention were published in the Savannah Georgian in 1828. In them he wrote incisive character sketches that are especially valuable for the information they provide about the lesser-known delegates.

## The Founding Fathers: Maryland

## Daniel Carroll, Maryland

Daniel Carroll was member of a prominent Maryland family of Irish descent. A collateral branch was led by Charles Carroll of Carrollton, signer of the Declaration of Independence. Daniel's older brother was John Carroll, the first Roman Catholic bishop in the United States.

Daniel was born in 1730 at Upper Marlboro, MD. Befitting the son of a wealthy Roman Catholic family, he studied for six years (1742-48) under the Jesuits at St. Omer's in Flanders. Then, after a tour of Europe, he sailed home and soon married Eleanor Carroll, apparently a first cousin of Charles Carroll of Carrollton. Not much is known about the next two decades of his life except that he backed the War for Independence reluctantly and remained out of the public eye. No doubt he lived the life of a gentleman planter.

In 1781 Carroll entered the political arena. Elected to the Continental Congress that year, he carried to Philadelphia the news that Maryland was at last ready to accede to the Articles of Confederation, to which he soon penned his name. During the decade, he also began a tour in the Maryland senate that was to span his lifetime and helped George Washington promote the Patowmack Company, a scheme to canalize the Potomac River so as to provide a transportation link between the East and the trans-Appalachian West.

Carroll did not arrive at the Constitutional Convention until July 9, but thereafter he attended quite regularly. He spoke about 20 times during the debates and served on the Committee on Postponed Matters. Returning to Maryland after the convention, he campaigned for ratification of the Constitution but was not a delegate to the state convention.

In 1789 Carroll won a seat in the U.S. House of Representatives, where he voted for locating the Nation's Capital on the banks of the Potomac and for Hamilton's program for the federal assumption of state debts. In 1791 George Washington named his friend Carroll as one of three commissioners to survey and define the District of Columbia, where Carroll owned much land. Ill health caused him to resign this post four years later, and the next year at the age of 65 he died at his home near Rock Creek in Forest Glen, MD. He was buried there in St. John's Catholic Cemetery.

## Daniel of St. Thomas Jenifer, Maryland

Jenifer was born in 1723 of Swedish and English descent at Coates Retirement (now Ellerslie) estate, near Port Tobacco in Charles County, Md. Little is known about his childhood or education, but as an adult he came into possession of a large estate near Annapolis, called Stepney, where he lived most of his life. He never married. The web of his far-reaching friendships included such illustrious personages as George Washington.

As a young man, Jenifer served as agent and receiver-general for the last two proprietors of Maryland. He also filled the post of justice of the peace in Charles County and later for the western circuit of Maryland. In 1760 he sat on a boundary commission that settled disputes between Pennsylvania and Delaware. Six years later, he became a member of the provincial court and from 1773 to 1776 sat on the Maryland royal governor's council.

Despite his association with conservative proprietary politics, Jenifer supported the Revolutionary movement, albeit at first reluctantly. He served as president of the Maryland council of safety (1775-77), then as president of the first state senate (1777-80). He sat in the Continental Congress (1778-82) and held the position of state revenue and financial manager (1782-85).

A conservative nationalist, Jenifer favored a strong and permanent union of the states and a Congress with taxation power. In 1785 he represented Maryland at the Mount Vernon Conference. Although he was one of 29 delegates who attended nearly every session of the Constitutional Convention, he did not speak often, but backed Madison and the nationalist element.

Jenifer lived only three more years and never again held public office. He died at the age of 66 or 67 at Annapolis in 1790. The exact location of his grave, possibly at Ellerslie estate, is unknown.

**Luther Martin, Maryland**

Like many of the delegates to the Constitutional Convention, Luther Martin attended the College of New Jersey (later Princeton), from which he graduated with honors in 1766. Though born in Brunswick, NJ., in 1748, Martin moved to Maryland after receiving his degree and taught there for three years. He then began to study the law and was admitted to the Virginia bar in 1771.

Martin was an early advocate of American independence from Great Britain. In the fall of 1774 he served on the patriot committee of Somerset County, and in December he attended a convention of the Province of Maryland in Annapolis, which had been called to consider the recommendations of the Continental Congress. Maryland appointed Luther Martin its attorney general in early 1778. In this capacity, Martin vigorously prosecuted

Loyalists, whose numbers were strong in many areas. Tensions had even led to insurrection and open warfare in some counties. While still attorney general, Martin joined the Baltimore Light Dragoons. In July 1781 his unit joined Lafayette's forces near Fredericksburg, VA., but Martin was recalled by the governor to prosecute a treason trial.

Martin married Maria Cresap on Christmas Day 1783. Of their five children, three daughters lived to adulthood. His postwar law practice grew to become one of the largest and most successful in the country. In 1785 Martin was elected to the Continental Congress, but this appointment was purely honorary. His numerous public and private duties prevented him from traveling to Philadelphia.

At the Constitutional Convention Martin opposed the idea of a strong central government. When he arrived on June 9, 1787, he expressed suspicion of the secrecy rule imposed on the proceedings. He consistently sided with the small states and voted against the Virginia Plan. On June 27 Martin spoke for more than three hours in opposition to the Virginia Plan's proposal for proportionate representation in both houses of the legislature. Martin served on the committee formed to seek a compromise on representation, where he supported the case for equal numbers of delegates in at least one house. Before the convention closed, he and another Maryland delegate, John Francis Mercer, walked out.

In an address to the Maryland House of Delegates in 1787 and in numerous newspaper articles, Martin attacked the proposed new form of government and continued to fight ratification of the Constitution through 1788. He lamented the ascension of the national government over the states and condemned what he saw as unequal representation in Congress. Martin opposed including slaves in determining representation and believed that the absence of a jury in the Supreme Court gravely endangered freedom. At the convention, Martin complained, the aggrandizement of particular states and individuals often had been pursued more avidly than the welfare of the country. The assumption of the term "federal" by those who favored a national government also irritated Martin. Around 1791, however, Martin turned to the Federalist party because of his animosity toward Thomas Jefferson.

The first years of the 1800s saw Martin as defense counsel in two controversial national cases. In the first Martin won an acquittal for his close friend, Supreme Court Justice Samuel Chase, in his impeachment trial in 1805. Two years later Martin was one of Aaron Burr's defense lawyers when Burr stood trial for treason in 1807.

After a record 28 consecutive years as state attorney general, Luther Martin resigned in December 1805. In 1813 Martin became chief judge of the court of oyer and terminer for the City and County of Baltimore. He was reappointed attorney general of Maryland in 1818, and in 1819 he argued Maryland's position in the landmark Supreme Court case McCulloch v. Maryland. The plaintiff, represented by Daniel Webster, William Pinckney, and William Wirt, won the decision, which determined that states could not tax federal institutions.

Martin's fortunes declined dramatically in his last years. Heavy drinking, illness, and poverty all took their toll. Paralysis, which had struck in 1819, forced him to retire as Maryland's attorney general in 1822. In 1826, at the age of 78, Luther Martin died in Aaron Burr's home in New York City and was buried in an unmarked grave in St. John's churchyard.

**James McHenry, Maryland**

McHenry was born in Ballymena, County Antrim, Ireland, in 1753. He enjoyed a classical education at Dublin, and emigrated to Philadelphia in 1771. The following year, the rest of his family came to the colonies, and his brother and father established an import business at Baltimore. During that year, James continued schooling at Newark Academy in Delaware and then studied medicine for two years under the well-known Dr. Benjamin Rush in Philadelphia.

During the War for Independence, McHenry served as a military surgeon. Late in 1776, while he was on the staff of the 5th Pennsylvania Battalion, the British captured him at Fort Washington, NY. He was paroled early the next year and exchanged in March 1778. Returning immediately to duty, he was assigned to Valley Forge, PA, and in May became secretary to George Washington. About this time, McHenry apparently quit the practice of medicine to devote himself to politics and administration; he apparently never needed to return to it after the war because of his excellent financial circumstances.

McHenry stayed on Washington's staff until 1780, when he joined that of the Marquis de Lafayette, and he remained in that assignment until he entered the Maryland Senate (1781-86). During part of this period, he served concurrently in the Continental Congress (1783-86). In 1784 he married Margaret Allison Caldwell.

McHenry missed many of the proceedings at the Philadelphia convention, in part because of the illness of his brother, and played an insubstantial part in the debates when he was present. He did, however, maintain a private journal that has been useful to posterity. He campaigned strenuously for the Constitution in Maryland and attended the state ratifying convention.

From 1789 to 1791, McHenry sat in the state assembly and in the years 1791-96 again in the senate. A staunch Federalist, he then accepted Washington's offer of the post of Secretary of War and held it into the administration of John Adams. McHenry looked to Hamilton rather than to Adams for leadership. As time passed, the latter became increasingly dissatisfied with McHenry's performance and distrustful of his political motives and in 1800 forced him to resign. Subsequently, the Democratic-Republicans accused him of maladministration, but a congressional committee vindicated him.

McHenry returned to his estate near Baltimore and to semiretirement. He remained a loyal Federalist and opposed the War of 1812. He also held the office of president of a Bible society. He died in 1816 at the age of 62, survived by two of his three children. His grave is in Baltimore's Westminster Presbyterian Cemetery.

### John Francis Mercer, Maryland

John Francis Mercer, born on May 17, 1759, was the fifth of nine children born to John and Ann Mercer of Stafford County, VA. He attended the College of William and Mary, and in early 1776 he joined the 3d Virginia Regiment. Mercer became Gen. Charles Lee's aide-decamp in 1778, but after General Lee's court-martial in October 1779, Mercer resigned his commission. He spent the next year studying law at the College of William and Mary and then rejoined the army, where he served briefly under Lafayette.

In 1782 Mercer was elected to the Virginia House of Delegates. That December he became one of Virginia's representatives to the Continental Congress. He later returned to the House of Delegates in 1785 and 1786.

Mercer married Sophia Sprigg in 1785 and soon after moved to Anne Arundel County, MD. He attended the Constitutional Convention as part of Maryland's delegation when he was only 28 years old, the second youngest delegate in Philadelphia. Mercer was strongly opposed to centralization, and both spoke and voted against the Constitution. He and fellow Marylander Luther Martin left the proceedings before they ended.

After the convention, Mercer continued in public service. He allied himself with the Republicans and served in the Maryland House of Delegates in 1778-89, 1791-92, 1800-1801, and 1803-6. Between 1791 and 1794 he also sat in the U.S. House of Representatives for Maryland and was chosen governor of the state for two terms, 1801-3. During Thomas Jefferson's term as President, Mercer broke with the Republicans and joined the Federalist camp.

Illness plagued him during his last years. In 1821 Mercer traveled to Philadelphia to seek medical attention, and he died there on August 30. His remains lay temporarily in a vault in St. Peter's Church in Philadelphia and were reinterred on his estate, "Cedar Park" in Maryland.

## The Founding Fathers: Massachusetts

### Elbridge Gerry, Massachusetts

Gerry was born in 1744 at Marblehead, MA, the third of 12 children. His mother was the daughter of a Boston merchant; his father, a wealthy and politically active merchant-shipper who had once been a sea captain. Upon graduating from Harvard in 1762, Gerry joined his father and two brothers in the family business, exporting dried codfish to Barbados and Spain. He entered the colonial legislature (1772-74), where he came under the influence of Samuel Adams, and took part in the Marblehead and Massachusetts committees of correspondence. When Parliament closed Boston harbor in June 1774, Marblehead became a major port of entry for supplies donated by patriots throughout the colonies to relieve Bostonians, and Gerry helped transport the goods.

Between 1774 and 1776 Gerry attended the first and second provincial congresses. He served with Samuel Adams and John Hancock on the council of safety and, as chairman of the committee of supply (a job for which his merchant background ideally suited him) wherein he raised troops and dealt with military logistics. On the night of April 18, 1775

Gerry attended a meeting of the council of safety at an inn in Menotomy (Arlington), between Cambridge and Lexington, and barely escaped the British troops marching on Lexington and Concord.

In 1776 Gerry entered the Continental Congress, where his congressional specialities were military and financial matters. In Congress and throughout his career his actions often appeared contradictory. He earned the nickname "soldiers' friend" for his advocacy of better pay and equipment, yet he vacillated on the issue of pensions. Despite his disapproval of standing armies, he recommended long-term enlistments.

Until 1779 Gerry sat on and sometimes presided over the congressional board that regulated Continental finances. After a quarrel over the price schedule for suppliers, Gerry, himself a supplier, walked out of Congress. Although nominally a member, he did not reappear for three years. During the interim, he engaged in trade and privateering and served in the lower house of the Massachusetts legislature.

As a representative in Congress in the years 1783-85, Gerry numbered among those who had possessed talent as Revolutionary agitators and wartime leaders but who could not effectually cope with the painstaking task of stabilizing the national government. He was experienced and conscientious but created many enemies with his lack of humor, suspicion of the motives of others, and obsessive fear of political and military tyranny. In 1786, the year after leaving Congress, he retired from business, married Ann Thompson, and took a seat in the state legislature.

Gerry was one of the most vocal delegates at the Constitutional Convention of 1787. He presided as chairman of the committee that produced the Great Compromise but disliked the compromise itself. He antagonized nearly everyone by his inconsistency and, according to a colleague, "objected to everything he did not propose." At first an advocate of a strong central government, Gerry ultimately rejected and refused to sign the Constitution because it lacked a bill of rights and because he deemed it a threat to republicanism. He led the drive against ratification in Massachusetts and denounced the document as "full of vices." Among the vices, he listed inadequate representation of the people, dangerously ambiguous legislative powers, the blending of the executive and the legislative, and the danger of an oppressive judiciary. Gerry did see some merit in the Constitution, though, and believed that its flaws could be remedied through amendments. In 1789, after he announced his intention to support the Constitution, he was elected to the First Congress where, to the chagrin of the Antifederalists, he championed Federalist policies.

Gerry left Congress for the last time in 1793 and retired for four years.

During this period he came to mistrust the aims of the Federalists, particularly their attempts to nurture an alliance with Britain, and sided with the pro-French Democratic-Republicans. In 1797 President John Adams appointed him as the only non-Federalist member of a three-man commission charged with negotiating a reconciliation with France, which was on the brink of war with the United States. During the ensuing XYZ affair (1797-98), Gerry tarnished his reputation. Talleyrand, the French foreign minister, led him to believe that his presence in France would prevent war, and Gerry lingered on long after the departure of John Marshall and Charles Cotesworth Pinckney, the two other commissioners. Finally, the embarrassed Adams recalled him, and Gerry met severe censure from the Federalists upon his return.

In 1800-1803 Gerry, never very popular among the Massachusetts electorate because of his aristocratic haughtiness, met defeat in four bids for the Massachusetts governorship but finally triumphed in 1810. Near the end of his two terms, scarred by partisan controversy, the Democratic-Republicans passed a redistricting measure to ensure their domination of the state senate. In response, the Federalists heaped ridicule on Gerry and coined the pun "gerrymander" to describe the salamander-like shape of one of the redistricted areas.

Despite his advanced age, frail health, and the threat of poverty brought on by neglect of personal affairs, Gerry served as James Madison's Vice President in 1813. In the fall of 1814, the 70-year old politician collapsed on his way to the Senate and died. He left his wife, who was to live until 1849, the last surviving widow of a signer of the Declaration of Independence, as well as three sons and four daughters. Gerry is buried in Congressional Cemetery at Washington, DC.

## Nathaniel Gorham, Massachusetts

Gorham, an eldest child, was born in 1738 at Charlestown, MA, into an old Bay Colony family of modest means. His father operated a packet boat. The youth's education was minimal. When he was about 15 years of age, he was apprenticed to a New London, CT, merchant. He quit in 1759, returned to his hometown and established a business which quickly succeeded. In 1763 he wed Rebecca Call, who was to bear nine children.

Gorham began his political career as a public notary but soon won election to the colonial legislature (1771-75). During the Revolution, he unswervingly backed the Whigs. He was a delegate to the provincial congress (1774-75), member of the Massachusetts Board of War (1778-81), delegate to the constitutional convention (1779-80), and representative in both the upper (1780) and lower (1781-87) houses of the legislature, including speaker of the latter in 1781, 1782, and 1785. In the last year, though he apparently lacked formal legal training, he began a judicial career as judge of the Middlesex County court of common pleas (1785-96). During this same period, he sat on the Governor's Council (1788-89).

During the war, British troops had ravaged much of Gorham's property, though by privateering and speculation he managed to recoup most of his fortune. Despite these pressing business concerns and his state political and judicial activities, he also served the nation. He was a member of the Continental Congress (1782-83 and 1785-87), and held the office of president from June 1786 until January 1787.

The next year, at age 49, Gorham attended the Constitutional Convention. A moderate nationalist, he attended all the sessions and played an influential role.. He spoke often, acted as chairman of the Committee of the Whole, and sat on the Committee of Detail. As a delegate to the Massachusetts ratifying convention, he stood behind the Constitution.

Some unhappy years followed. Gorham did not serve in the new government he had helped to create. In 1788 he and Oliver Phelps of Windsor, CT, and possibly others, contracted to purchase from the Commonwealth of Massachusetts six million acres of unimproved land in western New York. The price was $1 million in devalued Massachusetts scrip. Gorham and Phelps quickly succeeded in clearing Indian title to 2,600,000 acres in the eastern section of the grant and sold much of it to settlers. Problems soon arose, however. Massachusetts scrip rose dramatically in value, enormously swelling the purchase price of the vast tract. By 1790 the two men were unable to meet their payments. The result was a financial crisis that led to Gorham's insolvency - and a fall from the heights of Boston society and political esteem.

Gorham died in 1796 at the age of 58 and is buried at the Phipps Street Cemetery in Charlestown, MA.

## Rufus King, Massachusetts

King was born at Scarboro (Scarborough), MA (present Maine), in 1755. He was the eldest son of a prosperous farmer-merchant. At age 12, after receiving an elementary education at local schools, he matriculated at Dummer Academy in South Byfield, MA, and in 1777 graduated from Harvard. He served briefly as a general's aide during the War for Independence. Choosing a legal career, he read for the law at Newburyport, MA, and entered practice there in 1780.

King's knowledge, bearing, and oratorical gifts soon launched him on a political career. From 1783 to 1785 he was a member of the Massachusetts legislature, after which that body sent him to the Continental Congress (1784-86). There, he gained a reputation as a brilliant speaker and an early opponent of slavery. Toward the end of his tour, in 1786, he married Mary Alsop, daughter of a rich New York City merchant. He performed his final duties for Massachusetts by representing her at the Constitutional Convention and by serving in the commonwealth's ratifying convention.

At age 32, King was not only one of the most youthful of the delegates at Philadelphia, but was also one of the most important. He numbered among the most capable orators. Furthermore, he attended every session. Although he came to the convention unconvinced that major changes should be made in the Articles of Confederation, his views underwent a startling transformation during the debates. With Madison, he became a leading figure in the nationalist caucus. He served with distinction on the Committee on Postponed Matters and the Committee of Style. He also took notes on the proceedings, which have been valuable to historians.

About 1788 King abandoned his law practice, moved from the Bay State to Gotham, and entered the New York political forum. He was elected to the legislature (1789-90), and in the former year was picked as one of the state's first U.S. senators. As political divisions grew in the new government, King expressed ardent sympathies for the Federalists. In Congress, he supported Hamilton's fiscal program and stood among the leading proponents of the unpopular Jay's Treaty (1794).

Meantime, in 1791, King had become one of the directors of the First Bank of the United States. Reelected to the U.S. Senate in 1795, he served only a year before he was appointed as Minister to Great Britain (1796-1803).

King's years in this post were difficult ones in Anglo-American relations. The wars of the French Revolution endangered U.S. commerce in the maritime clashes between the French and the British. The latter in particular violated American rights on the high seas, especially by the impressment of sailors. Although King was unable to bring about a change in this policy, he smoothed relations between the two nations.

In 1803 King sailed back to the United States and to a career in politics. In 1804 and 1808 fellow-signer Charles Cotesworth Pinckney and he were the Federalist candidates for President and Vice President, respectively, but were decisively defeated. Otherwise, King largely contented himself with agricultural pursuits at King Manor, a Long Island estate he had purchased in 1805. During the War of 1812, he was again elected to the U.S. Senate (1813-25) and ranked as a leading critic of the war. Only after the British attacked Washington in 1814 did he come to believe that the United States was fighting a defensive action and to lend his support to the war effort.

In 1816 the Federalists chose King as their candidate for the presidency, but James Monroe beat him handily. Still in the Senate, that same year King led the opposition to the establishment of the Second Bank of the United States. Four years later, believing that the issue of slavery could not be compromised but must be settled once and for all by the immediate establishment of a system of compensated emancipation and colonization, he denounced the Missouri Compromise.

In 1825, suffering from ill health, King retired from the Senate. President John Quincy Adams, however, persuaded him to accept another assignment as Minister to Great Britain. He arrived in England that same year, but soon fell ill and was forced to return home the following year. Within a year, at the age of 72, in 1827, he died. Surviving him were several offspring, some of whom also gained distinction. He was laid to rest near King Manor in the cemetery of Grace Episcopal Church, Jamaica, Long Island, NY.

**Caleb Strong, Massachusetts**

Strong was born to Caleb and Phebe Strong on January 9, 1745 in Northampton, MA. He received his college education at Harvard, from which he graduated with highest honors in 1764. Like so many of the delegates to the Constitutional Convention, Strong chose to study law and was admitted to the bar in 1772. He enjoyed a prosperous country practice.

From 1774 through the duration of the Revolution, Strong was a member of Northampton's committee of safety. In 1776 he was elected to the Massachusetts General Court and also held the post of county attorney for Hampshire County for 24 years. He was offered a position on the state supreme court in 1783 but declined it.

At the Constitutional Convention, Strong counted himself among the delegates who favored a strong central government. He successfully moved that the House of Representatives should originate all money bills and sat on the drafting committee. Though he preferred a system that accorded the same rank and mode of election to both houses of Congress, he voted in favor of equal representation in the Senate and proportional in the House. Strong was called home on account of illness in his family and so missed the opportunity to sign the Constitution. However, during the Massachusetts ratifying convention, he took a leading role among the Federalists and campaigned strongly for ratification.

Massachusetts chose Strong as one of its first U.S. senators in 1789. During the four years he served in that house, he sat on numerous committees and participated in framing the Judiciary Act. Caleb Strong wholeheartedly supported the Washington administration. In 1793 he urged the government to send a mission to England and backed the resulting Jay's Treaty when it met heated opposition.

Caleb Strong, the Federalist candidate, defeated Elbridge Gerry to become Governor of Massachusetts in 1800. Despite the growing strength of the Democratic party in the state, Strong won reelection annually until 1807. In 1812 he regained the governorship, once again over Gerry, and retained his post until he retired in 1816. During the War of 1812 Strong withstood pressure from the Secretary of War to order part of the Massachusetts militia into federal service. Strong opposed the war and approved the report of the Hartford Convention, a gathering of New England Federalists resentful of Jeffersonian policies.

Strong died on November 7, 1819, two years after the death of his wife, Sarah. He was buried in the Bridge Street Cemetery in Northampton. Four of his nine children survived him.

## The Founding Fathers: New Hampshire

### Nicholas Gilman, New Hampshire

As a member of a distinguished New Hampshire family and second son in a family of eight, Nicholas Gilman was born at Exeter in 1755. He received his education in local schools and worked at his father's general store.

When the War for Independence began, he enlisted in the New Hampshire element of the Continental Army, soon won a captaincy, and served throughout the war. Gilman returned home, again helped his father in the store, and immersed himself in politics. In the period 1786-88 he sat in the Continental Congress, though his attendance record was poor. In 1787 he represented New Hampshire at the Constitutional Convention. He did not arrive at Philadelphia until July 21, by which time much major business had already occurred. Never much of a debater, he made no speeches and played only a minor part in the deliberations. He did, however, serve on the Committee on Postponed Matters. He was also active in obtaining New Hampshire's acceptance of the Constitution and in shepherding it through the Continental Congress.

Gilman later became a prominent Federalist politician. He served in the U.S. House of Representatives from 1789 until 1797; and in 1793 and 1797 was a presidential elector. He also sat in the New Hampshire legislature in 1795, 1802, and 1804, and in the years 1805-8 and 1811-14 he held the office of state treasurer. Meantime, Gilman's political philosophy had begun to drift toward the Democratic-Republicans. In 1802, when he was defeated for the U.S. Senate, President Jefferson appointed him as a bankruptcy commissioner, and two years later as a Democratic-Republican he won election to the U.S. Senate. He was still serving there when he passed away at Philadelphia, while on his way home from Washington, DC, in 1814 at the age of 58. He is interred at the Winter Street Cemetery at Exeter.

## John Langdon, New Hampshire

Langdon was born in 1741 at or near Portsmouth, NH. His father, whose family had emigrated to America before 1660, was a prosperous farmer who sired a large family. The youth's education was intermittent. He attended a local grammar school, worked as an apprentice clerk, and spent some time at sea. Eventually he went into the mercantile business for himself and prospered. Langdon, a vigorous supporter of the Revolution, sat on the New Hampshire committee of correspondence and a nonimportation committee. He also attended various patriot assemblies. In 1774 he participated in the seizure and confiscation of British munitions from the Portsmouth fort. The next year, Langdon served as speaker of the New Hampshire assembly and also sat in the Continental Congress (1775-76). During the latter year, he accepted a colonelcy in the militia of his state and became its agent for British prizes on behalf of the Continental Congress, a post he held throughout the war. In addition, he built privateers for operations against the British - a lucrative occupation. Langdon also actively took part in the land war. In 1777 he organized and paid for Gen. John Stark's expedition from New Hampshire against British Gen. John Burgoyne and was present in command of a militia unit at Saratoga, NY, when the latter surrendered. Langdon later led a detachment of troops during the Rhode Island campaign, but found his major outlet in politics. He was speaker of the New Hampshire legislature from 1777 to 1781. In 1777, meantime, he had married Elizabeth Sherburne, who was to give birth to one daughter. In 1783 Langdon was elected to the Continental Congress; the next year, to the state senate; and the following year, as president, or chief executive, of New Hampshire. In 1784 he built a home at Portsmouth.

In 1786-87 he was back again as speaker of the legislature and during the latter year for the third time in the Continental Congress. Langdon was forced to pay his own expenses and those of Nicholas Gilman to the Constitutional Convention because New Hampshire was unable or unwilling to pay them. The pair did not arrive at Philadelphia until late July, by which time much business had already been consummated. Thereafter, Langdon made a significant mark. He spoke more than 20 times during the debates and was a member of the committee that struck a compromise on the issue of slavery. For the most part, his sympathies lay on the side of strengthening the national government. In 1788, once again as state president (1788-89), he took part in the ratifying convention. From 1789 to 1801 Langdon sat in the U.S. Senate, including service as the first President pro tem for several sessions. During these years, his political affiliations changed. As a supporter of a strong central government, he had been a member of the Federalist Party, but by the time of Jay's Treaty (1794) he was opposing its policies.

By 1801 he was firmly backing the Democratic-Republicans. That year, Langdon declined Jefferson's offer of the Secretaryship of the Navy. Between then and 1812, he kept active in New Hampshire politics. He sat again in the legislature (1801-5), twice holding the position of speaker. After several unsuccessful attempts, in 1805 he was elected as governor and continued in that post until 1811 except for a year's hiatus in 1809. Meanwhile, in 1805, Dartmouth College had awarded him an honorary doctor of laws degree. In 1812 Langdon refused the Democratic-Republican Vice-Presidential nomination on the grounds of age and health. He enjoyed retirement for another seven years before he died at the age of 78. His grave is at Old North Cemetery in Portsmouth.

## The Founding Fathers: New Jersey

## David Brearly, New Jersey

Brearly (Brearley) was descended from a Yorkshire, England, family, one of whose members migrated to New Jersey around 1680. Signer Brearly was born in 1745 at Spring Grove near Trenton, was reared in the area, and attended but did not graduate from the nearby College of New Jersey (later Princeton). He chose law as a career and originally practiced at Allentown, NJ. About 1767 he married Elizabeth Mullen. Brearly avidly backed the Revolutionary cause. The British arrested him for high treason, but a group of patriots freed him. In 1776 he took part in the convention that drew up the state constitution. During the War for Independence, he rose from a captain to a colonel in the militia. In 1779 Brearly was elected as chief justice of the New Jersey supreme court, a position he held until 1789. He presided over the precedent-setting case of Holmes v. Walton. His decision, rendered in 1780, represented an early expression of the principle of judicial review. The next year, the College of New Jersey bestowed an honorary M.A. degree on him. Brearly was 42 years of age when he participated in the Constitutional Convention.

Although he did not rank among the leaders, he attended the sessions regularly. A follower of Paterson, who introduced the New Jersey Plan, Brearly opposed proportional representation of the states and favored one vote for each of them in Congress. He also chaired the Committee on Postponed Matters. Brearly's subsequent career was short, for he had only three years to live. He presided at the New Jersey convention that ratified the Constitution in 1788, and served as a presidential elector in 1789. That same year, President Washington appointed him as a federal district judge, and he served in that capacity until his death. When free from his judicial duties, Brearly devoted much energy to lodge and church affairs. He was one of the leading members of the Masonic Order in New Jersey, as well as state vice president of the Society of the Cincinnati, an organization of former officers of the Revolutionary War. In addition, he served as a delegate to the Episcopal General Conference (1786) and helped write the church's prayer book. In 1783, following the death of his first wife, he had married Elizabeth Higbee. Brearly died in Trenton at the age of 45 in 1790. He was buried there at St. Michael's Episcopal Church.

## Jonathan Dayton, New Jersey

Dayton was born at Elizabethtown (present Elizabeth), NJ, in 1760. His father was a storekeeper who was also active in local and state politics. The youth obtained a good education, graduating from the College of New Jersey (later Princeton) in 1776. He immediately entered the Continental Army and saw extensive action. Achieving the rank of captain by the age of 19 and serving under his father, Gen. Elias Dayton, and the Marquis de Lafayette, he was a prisoner of the British for a time and participated in the Battle of Yorktown, VA.

After the war, Dayton returned home, studied law, and established a practice. During the 1780s he divided his time between land speculation, legal practice, and politics. He sat in the assembly in 1786-87. In the latter year, he was chosen as a delegate to the Constitutional Convention after the leaders of his political faction, his father and his patron, Abraham Clark, declined to attend. Dayton did not arrive at Philadelphia until June 21 but thereafter faithfully took part in the proceedings. He spoke with moderate frequency during the debates and, though objecting to some provisions of the Constitution, signed it.

After sitting in the Continental Congress in 1788, Dayton became a foremost Federalist legislator in the new government. Although elected as a representative, he did not serve in the First Congress in 1789, preferring instead to become a member of the New Jersey council and speaker of the state assembly. In 1791, however, he entered the U.S. House of Representatives (1791-99), becoming Speaker in the Fourth and Fifth Congresses. During this period, he backed Hamilton's fiscal program, suppression of the Whisky Rebellion, Jay's Treaty, and a host of other Federalist measures.

In personal matters Dayton purchased Boxwood Hall in 1795 as his home in Elizabethtown and resided there until his death. He was elevated to the U.S. Senate (1799-1805). He supported the Louisiana Purchase (1803) and, in conformance with his Federalist views, opposed the repeal of the Judiciary Act of 1801.

In 1806 illness prevented Dayton from accompanying Aaron Burr's abortive expedition to the Southwest, where the latter apparently intended to conquer Spanish lands and create an empire. Subsequently indicted for treason, Dayton was not prosecuted but could not salvage his national political career. He remained popular in New Jersey, however, continuing to hold local offices and sitting in the assembly (1814-15).

In 1824 the 63-year-old Dayton played host to Lafayette during his triumphal tour of the United States, and his death at Elizabeth later that year may have been hastened by the exertion and excitement. He was laid to rest at St. John's Episcopal Church in his hometown. Because he owned 250,000 acres of Ohio land between the Big and Little Miami Rivers, the city of Dayton, was named after him - his major monument. He had married Susan Williamson, but the date of their wedding is unknown. They had two daughters.

## William C. Houston, New Jersey

William Houston was born about 1746 to Margaret and Archibald Houston. He attended the College of New Jersey (later Princeton) and graduated in 1768 and became master of the college grammar school and then its tutor. In 1771 he was appointed professor of mathematics and natural philosophy.

From 1775 to 1776 Houston was deputy secretary of the Continental Congress. He also saw active military service in 1776 and 1777 when, as captain of the foot militia of Somerset County, he engaged in action around Princeton. During the Revolution, Houston also served in the New Jersey Assembly (1777) and the New Jersey Council of Safety (1778). In 1779 he was once again elected to the Continental Congress, where he worked mainly in the areas of supply and finance. In addition to serving in Congress, Houston remained active in the affairs of the College of New Jersey and also found time to study law. He was admitted to the bar in 1781 and won the appointment of clerk of the New Jersey Supreme Court in the same year. Houston resigned from the college in 1783 and concentrated on his Trenton law practice. He represented New Jersey in Congress once again in 1784 and 1785.

Houston represented New Jersey at both the Annapolis and Philadelphia conventions. Though illness forced him to leave after one week, he did serve on a committee to consider the distribution of seats in the lower house. Houston did not sign the Constitution, but he signed the report to the New Jersey legislature.

On August 12, 1788, William Houston succumbed to tuberculosis and died in Frankford, PA., leaving his wife Jane, two daughters, and two sons. His body was laid to rest in the Second Presbyterian Churchyard in Philadelphia.

## William Livingston, New Jersey

Livingston was born in 1723 at Albany, NY. His maternal grandmother reared him until he was 14, and he then spent a year with a missionary among the Mohawk Indians. He attended Yale and graduated in 1741.

Rejecting his family's hope that he would enter the fur trade at Albany or mercantile pursuits in New York City, young Livingston chose to pursue a career in law at the latter place. Before he completed his legal studies, in 1745 he married Susanna French, daughter of a well-to-do New Jersey landowner. She was to bear 13 children.

Three years later, Livingston was admitted to the bar and quickly gained a reputation as the supporter of popular causes against the more conservative factions in the city. Associated with the Calvinists in religion, he opposed the dominant Anglican leaders in the colony and wielded a sharply satirical pen in verses and broadsides. Livingston attacked the Anglican attempt to charter and control King's College (later Columbia College and University) and the dominant De Lancey party for its Anglican sympathies, and by 1758 rose to the leadership of his faction. For a decade, it controlled the colonial assembly and fought against parliamentary interference in the colony's affairs. During this time, 1759-61, Livingston sat in the assembly.

In 1769 Livingston's supporters, split by the growing debate as to how to respond to British taxation of the colonies, lost control of the assembly. Not long thereafter, Livingston, who had also grown tired of legal practice, moved to the Elizabethtown (present Elizabeth), NJ, area, where he had purchased land in 1760. There, in 1772-73, he built the estate, Liberty Hall, continued to write verse, and planned to live the life of a gentleman farmer.

The Revolutionary upsurge, however, brought Livingston out of retirement. He soon became a member of the Essex County, NJ, committee of correspondence; in 1774 a representative in the First Continental Congress; and in 1775-76 a delegate to the Second Continental Congress. In June 1776 he left Congress to command the New Jersey militia as a brigadier general and held this post until he was elected later in the year as the first governor of the state.

Livingston held the position throughout and beyond the war - in fact, for 14 consecutive years until his death in 1790. During his administration, the government was organized, the war won, and New Jersey launched on her path as a sovereign state. Although the pressure of affairs often prevented it, he enjoyed his estate whenever possible, conducted agricultural experiments, and became a member of the Philadelphia Society for Promoting Agriculture. He was also active in the antislavery movement.

In 1787 Livingston was selected as a delegate to the Constitutional Convention, though his gubernatorial duties prevented him from attending every session. He did not arrive until June 5th and missed several weeks in July, but he performed vital committee work, particularly as chairman of the one that reached a compromise on the issue of slavery. He also supported the New Jersey Plan. In addition, he spurred New Jersey's rapid ratification of the Constitution (1787). The next year, Yale awarded him an honorary doctor of laws degree.

Livingston died at Liberty Hall in his 67th year in 1790. He was originally buried at the local Presbyterian Churchyard, but a year later his remains were moved to a vault his son owned at Trinity Churchyard in Manhattan and in 1844 were again relocated, to Brooklyn's Greenwood Cemetery.

## William Paterson, New Jersey

William Paterson (Patterson) was born in County Antrim, Ireland, in 1745. When he was almost two years of age, his family emigrated to America, disembarking at New Castle, DE. While the father traveled about the country, apparently selling tinware, the family lived in New London, other places in Connecticut, and in Trenton, NJ. In 1750 he settled in Princeton, NJ. There, he became a merchant and manufacturer of tin goods. His prosperity enabled William to attend local private schools and the College of New Jersey (later Princeton). He took a B.A. in 1763 and an M.A. three years later.

Meantime, Paterson had studied law in the city of Princeton under Richard Stockton, who later was to sign the Declaration of Independence, and near the end of the decade began practicing at New Bromley, in Hunterdon County. Before long, he moved to South Branch, in Somerset County, and then in 1779 relocated near New Brunswick at Raritan estate.

When the War for Independence broke out, Paterson joined the vanguard of the New Jersey patriots. He served in the provincial congress (1775-76), the constitutional convention (1776), legislative council (1776-77), and council of safety (1777). During the last year, he also held a militia commission. From 1776 to 1783 he was attorney general of New Jersey, a task that occupied so much of his time that it prevented him from accepting election to the Continental Congress in 1780. Meantime, the year before, he had married Cornelia Bell, by whom he had three children before her death in 1783. Two years later, he took a new bride, Euphemia White, but it is not known whether or not they had children.

From 1783, when he moved into the city of New Brunswick, until 1787, Paterson devoted his energies to the law and stayed out of the public limelight. Then he was chosen to represent New Jersey at the Constitutional Convention, which he attended only until late July. Until then, he took notes of the proceedings. More importantly, he figured prominently because of his advocacy and coauthorship of the New Jersey, or Paterson, Plan, which asserted the rights of the small states against the large. He apparently returned to the convention only to sign the final document. After supporting its ratification in New Jersey, he began a career in the new government.

In 1789 Paterson was elected to the U.S. Senate (1789-90), where he played a pivotal role in drafting the Judiciary Act of 1789. His next position was governor of his state (1790-93). During this time, he began work on the volume later published as Laws of the State of New Jersey (1800) and began to revise the rules and practices of the chancery and common law courts.

During the years 1793-1806, Paterson served as an associate justice of the U.S. Supreme Court. Riding the grueling circuit to which federal judges were subjected in those days and sitting with the full Court, he presided over a number of major trials.

In September 1806, his health failing, the 60-year-old Paterson embarked on a journey to Ballston Spa, NY, for a cure but died en route at Albany in the home of his daughter, who had married Stephen Van Rensselaer. Paterson was at first laid to rest in the nearby Van Rensselaer manor house family vault, but later his body was apparently moved to the Albany Rural Cemetery, Menands, NY.

## The Founding Fathers: New York

### Alexander Hamilton, New York

Hamilton was born in 1757 on the island of Nevis, in the Leeward group, British West Indies. He was the illegitimate son of a common-law marriage between a poor itinerant Scottish merchant of aristocratic descent and an English-French Huguenot mother who was a planter's daughter. In 1766, after the father had moved his family elsewhere in the Leewards to St. Croix in the Danish (now United States) Virgin Islands, he returned to St. Kitts while his wife and two sons remained on St. Croix.

The mother, who opened a small store to make ends meet, and a Presbyterian clergyman provided Hamilton with a basic education, and he learned to speak fluent French. About the time of his mother's death in 1768, he became an apprentice clerk at Christiansted in a mercantile establishment, whose proprietor became one of his benefactors. Recognizing his ambition and superior intelligence, they raised a fund for his education.

In 1772, bearing letters of introduction, Hamilton traveled to New York City. Patrons he met there arranged for him to attend Barber's Academy at Elizabethtown (present Elizabeth), NJ. During this time, he met and stayed for a while at the home of William Livingston, who would one day be a fellow signer of the Constitution. Late the next year, 1773, Hamilton entered King's College (later Columbia College and University) in New York City, but the Revolution interrupted his studies.

Although not yet 20 years of age, in 1774-75 Hamilton wrote several widely read pro-Whig pamphlets. Right after the war broke out, he accepted an artillery captaincy and fought in the principal campaigns of 1776-77. In the latter year, winning the rank of lieutenant colonel, he joined the staff of General Washington as secretary and aide-de-camp and soon became his close confidant as well.

In 1780 Hamilton wed New Yorker Elizabeth Schuyler, whose family was rich and politically powerful; they were to have eight children. In 1781, after some disagreements with Washington, he took a command position under Lafayette in the Yorktown, VA, campaign (1781). He resigned his commission that November.

Hamilton then read law at Albany and quickly entered practice, but public service soon attracted him. He was elected to the Continental Congress in 1782-83. In the latter year, he established a law office in New York City. Because of his interest in strengthening the central government, he represented his state at the Annapolis Convention in 1786, where he urged the calling of the Constitutional Convention.

In 1787 Hamilton served in the legislature, which appointed him as a delegate to the convention. He played a surprisingly small part in the debates, apparently because he was frequently absent on legal business, his extreme nationalism put him at odds with most of the delegates, and he was frustrated by the conservative views of his two fellow delegates from New York. He did, however, sit on the Committee of Style, and he was the only one of the three delegates from his state who signed the finished document. Hamilton's part in New York's ratification the next year was substantial, though he felt the Constitution was deficient in many respects. Against determined opposition, he waged a strenuous and successful campaign, including collaboration with John Jay and James Madison in writing The Federalist. In 1787 Hamilton was again elected to the Continental Congress.

When the new government got under way in 1789, Hamilton won the position of Secretary of the Treasury. He began at once to place the nation's disorganized finances on a sound footing. In a series of reports (1790-91), he presented a program not only to stabilize national finances but also to shape the future of the country as a powerful, industrial nation. He proposed establishment of a national bank, funding of the national debt, assumption of state war debts, and the encouragement of manufacturing.

Hamilton's policies soon brought him into conflict with Jefferson and Madison. Their disputes with him over his pro-business economic program, sympathies for Great Britain, disdain for the common man, and opposition to the principles and excesses of the French revolution contributed to the formation of the first U.S. party system. It pitted Hamilton and the Federalists against Jefferson and Madison and the Democratic-Republicans.

During most of the Washington administration, Hamilton's views usually prevailed with the President, especially after 1793 when Jefferson left the government. In 1795 family and financial needs forced Hamilton to resign from the Treasury Department and resume his law practice in New York City. Except for a stint as inspector-general of the Army (1798-1800) during the undeclared war with France, he never again held public office.

While gaining stature in the law, Hamilton continued to exert a powerful impact on New York and national politics. Always an opponent of fellow-Federalist John Adams, he sought to prevent his election to the presidency in 1796. When that failed, he continued to use his influence secretly within Adams' cabinet. The bitterness between the two men became public knowledge in 1800 when Hamilton denounced Adams in a letter that was published through the efforts of the Democratic-Republicans.

In 1802 Hamilton and his family moved into The Grange, a country home he had built in a rural part of Manhattan not far north of New York City. But the expenses involved and investments in northern land speculations seriously strained his finances.

Meanwhile, when Jefferson and Aaron Burr tied in Presidential electoral votes in 1800, Hamilton threw valuable support to Jefferson. In 1804, when Burr sought the governorship of New York, Hamilton again managed to defeat him. That same year, Burr, taking offense at remarks he believed to have originated with Hamilton, challenged him to a duel, which took place at present Weehawken, NJ, on July 11. Mortally wounded, Hamilton died the next day. He was in his late forties at death. He was buried in Trinity Churchyard in New York City.

### John Lansing, Jr., New York

On January 30, 1754, John Lansing was born in Albany, NY, to Gerrit Jacob and Jannetje Lansing. At age 21 Lansing had completed his study of the law and was admitted to practice. In 1781 he married Cornelia Ray. They had 10 children, five of whom died in infancy. Lansing was quite wealthy; he owned a large estate at Lansingburg and had a lucrative law practice.

From 1776 to 1777 Lansing acted as military secretary to Gen. Philip Schuyler. From the military world Lansing turned to the political and served six terms in the New York Assembly - 1780-84, 1786, and 1788. During the last two terms he was speaker of the assembly. In the 2-year gap between his first four terms in the assembly and the fifth, Lansing sat in the Confederation Congress. He rounded out his public service by serving as Albany's mayor between 1786 and 1790.

Lansing went to Philadelphia as part of the New York delegation to the

Constitutional Convention. As the convention progressed, Lansing became disillusioned because he believed it was exceeding its instructions. Lansing believed the delegates had gathered together simply to amend the Articles of Confederation and was dismayed at the movement to write an entirely new constitution. After six weeks, John Lansing and fellow New York delegate Robert Yates left the convention and explained their departure in a joint letter to New York Governor George Clinton. They stated that they opposed any system that would consolidate the United States into one government, and they had understood that the convention would not consider any such consolidation. Furthermore, warned Lansing and Yates, the kind of government recommended by the convention could not "afford that security to equal and permanent liberty which we wished to make an invariable object of our pursuit." In 1788, as a member of the New York ratifying convention, Lansing again vigorously opposed the Constitution.

Under the new federal government Lansing pursued a long judicial career. In 1790 he began an 11-year term on the supreme court of New York; from 1798 until 1801 he served as its chief justice. Between 1801 and 1814 Lansing was chancellor of the state. Retirement from that post did not slow him down; in 1817 he accepted an appointment as a regent of the University of the State of New York.

Lansing's death was the most mysterious of all the delegates to the Constitutional Convention. While on a visit to New York City in 1829, he left his hotel to post some letters. No trace of him was ever found, and it was supposed that he had been murdered.

**Robert Yates, New York**

The son of Joseph and Maria Yates, Robert Yates was born in Schenectady, NY, on January 27, 1738. He received a classical education in New York City and later studied law with William Livingston. Yates was admitted to the New York bar in 1760 and thereafter resided in Albany.

Between 1771 and 1775 Yates sat on the Albany board of aldermen. During the pre-Revolution years Yates counted himself among the Radical Whigs, whose vigilance against corruption and emphasis on the protection of liberty in England appealed to many in the colonies. Once the Revolution broke out, Yates served on the Albany committee of safety and represented his county in four provincial congresses and in the convention of 1775-77. At the convention he sat on various committees, including the one that drafted the first constitution for New York State.

On May 8, 1777, Yates was appointed to New York's supreme court and presided as its chief justice from 1790 through 1798. While on the bench he attracted criticism for his fair treatment of Loyalists. Other duties included serving on commissions that were called to settle boundary disputes with Massachusetts and Vermont.

In the 1780's Robert Yates stood as a recognized leader of the Antifederalists. He opposed any concessions to the federal congress, such as the right to collect impost duties, that might diminish the sovereignty of the states. When he travelled to Philadelphia in May 1787 for the federal convention, he expected that the delegates would simply discuss revising the existing Articles. Yates was on the committee that debated the question of representation in the legislature, and it soon became apparent that the convention intended much more than modification of the current plan of union. On July 5, the day the committee presented its report, Yates and John Lansing (to whom Yates was related by marriage) left the proceedings. In a joint letter to Gov. George Clinton of New York, they spelled out the reasons for their early departure. They warned against the dangers of centralizing power and urged opposition to adopting the Constitution. Yates continued to attack the Constitution in a series of letters signed "Brutus" and "Sydney" and voted against ratification at the Poughkeepsie convention.

In 1789 Yates ran for governor of New York but lost the election. Three years after his retirement from the state supreme court, on September 9, 1801, he died, leaving his wife, Jannetje Van Ness Yates, and four of his six children. Though he had enjoyed a comfortable income at the start of his career, his capital had dwindled away until very little was left. In 1821 his notes from the Constitutional Convention were published under the title Secret Proceedings and Debates of the Convention Assembled . . . for the Purpose of Forming the Constitution of the United States.

## The Founding Fathers: North Carolina

### William Blount, North Carolina

William Blount was the great-grandson of Thomas Blount, who came from England to Virginia soon after 1660 and settled on a North Carolina plantation. William, the eldest in a large family, was born in 1749 while his mother was visiting his grandfather's Rosefield estate, on the site of present Windsor near Pamlico Sound. The youth apparently received a good education.

Shortly after the War for Independence began, in 1776, Blount enlisted as a paymaster in the North Carolina forces. Two years later, he wed Mary Grainier (Granger); of their six children who reached adulthood, one son also became prominent in Tennessee politics.

Blount spent most of the remainder of his life in public office. He sat in the lower house of the North Carolina legislature (1780-84), including service as speaker, as well as in the upper (1788-90). In addition, he took part in national politics, serving in the Continental Congress in 1782-83 and 1786-87.

Appointed as a delegate to the Constitutional Convention at the age of 38, Blount was absent for more than a month because he chose to attend the Continental Congress on behalf of his state. He said almost nothing in the debates and signed the Constitution reluctantly - only, he said, to make it "the unanimous act of the States in Convention." Nonetheless, he favored his state's ratification of the completed document.

Blount hoped to be elected to the first U.S. Senate. When he failed to achieve that end, in 1790 he pushed westward beyond the Appalachians, where he held speculative land interests and had represented North Carolina in dealings with the Indians. He settled in what became Tennessee, to which he devoted the rest of his life. He resided first at Rocky Mount, a cabin near present Johnson City and in 1792 built a mansion in Knoxville.

Two years earlier, Washington had appointed Blount as Governor for the Territory South of the River Ohio (which included Tennessee) and also as Superintendent of Indian Affairs for the Southern Department, in which positions he increased his popularity with the frontiersmen. In 1796 he presided over the constitutional convention that transformed part of the territory into the State of Tennessee. He was elected as one of its first U.S. senators (1796-97).

During this period, Blount's affairs took a sharp turn for the worse. In 1797 his speculations in western lands led him into serious financial difficulties. That same year, he also apparently concocted a plan involving use of Indians, frontiersmen, and British naval forces to conquer for Britain the Spanish provinces of Florida and Louisiana. A letter he wrote alluding to the plan fell into the hands of President Adams, who turned it over to the Senate on July 3, 1797. Five days later, that body voted 25 to one to expel Blount. The House impeached him, but the Senate dropped the charges in 1799 on the grounds that no further action could be taken beyond his dismissal.

The episode did not hamper Blount's career in Tennessee. In 1798 he was elected to the senate and rose to the speakership. He died two years later at Knoxville in his early fifties. He is buried there in the cemetery of the First Presbyterian Church.

## William Richardson Davie, North Carolina

One of the eight delegates born outside of the thirteen colonies, Davie was born in Egremont, Cumberlandshire, England, on June 20, 1756. In 1763 Archibald Davie brought his son William to Waxhaw, SC.. Davie attended Queen's Museum College in Charlotte, North Carolina, and graduated from the College of New Jersey (later Princeton) in 1776.

Davie's law studies in Salisbury, NC, were interrupted by military service, but he won his license to practice before county courts in 1779 and in the superior courts in 1780. When the War for Independence broke out, he helped raise a troop of cavalry near Salisbury and eventually achieved the rank of colonel. While attached to Pulaski's division, Davie was wounded leading a charge at Stono, near Charleston, on June 20, 1779. Early in 1780 he raised another troop and operated mainly in western North Carolina. In January 1781 Davie was appointed commissary-general for the Carolina campaign. In this capacity he oversaw the collection of arms and supplies to Gen. Nathanael Greene's army and the state militia.

After the war, Davie embarked on his career as a lawyer, traveling the circuit in North Carolina. In 1782 he married Sarah Jones, the daughter of his former commander, Gen. Allen Jones, and settled in Halifax. His legal knowledge and ability won him great respect, and his presentation of arguments was admired. Between 1786 and 1798 Davie represented Halifax in the North Carolina legislature. There he was the principal agent behind that body's actions to revise and codify state laws, send representatives to the Annapolis and Philadelphia conventions, cede Tennessee to the Union, and fix disputed state boundaries.

During the Constitutional Convention Davie favored plans for a strong central government. He was a member of the committee that considered the question of representation in Congress and swung the North Carolina delegation's vote in favor of the Great Compromise. He favored election of senators and presidential electors by the legislature and insisted on counting slaves in determining representation. Though he left the convention on August 13, before its adjournment, Davie fought hard for the Constitution's ratification and took a prominent part in the North Carolina convention.

The political and military realms were not the only ones in which Davie left his mark. The University of North Carolina, of which he was the chief founder, stands as an enduring reminder of Davie's interest in education. Davie selected the location, instructors, and a curriculum that included the literary and social sciences as well as mathematics and classics. In 1810 the trustees conferred upon him the title of "Father of the University" and in the next year granted him the degree of Doctor of Laws.

Davie became Governor of North Carolina in 1798. His career also turned back briefly to the military when President John Adams appointed him a brigadier general in the U.S. Army that same year. Davie later served as a peace commissioner to France in 1799.

Davie stood as a candidate for Congress in 1803 but met defeat. In 1805, after the death of his wife, Davie retired from politics to his plantation, "Tivoli," in Chester County, South Carolina. In 1813 he declined an appointment as major-general from President Madison. Davie was 64 years old when he died on November 29, 1820, at "Tivoli," and he was buried in the Old Waxhaw Presbyterian Churchyard in northern Lancaster County.

## Alexander Martin, North Carolina

Though he represented North Carolina at the Constitutional Convention, Alexander Martin was born in Hunterdon County, NJ, in 1740. His parents, Hugh and Jane Martin, moved first to Virginia, then to Guilford County, NC, when Alexander was very young. Martin attended the College of New Jersey (later Princeton), received his degree in 1756, and moved to Salisbury. There he started his career as a merchant but turned to public service as he became justice of the peace, deputy king's attorney, and, in 1774 and 1775, judge of Salisbury district.

At the September 1770 session of the superior court at Hillsboro, 150 Regulators armed with sticks, switches, and cudgels crowded into the courtroom. They had come to present a petition to the judge demanding unprejudiced juries and a public accounting of taxes by sheriffs. Violence erupted, and several, including Alexander Martin, were beaten. In 1771 Martin signed an agreement with the Regulators to refund all fees taken illegally and to arbitrate all differences.

From 1773 to 1774 Martin served in the North Carolina House of Commons and in the second and third provincial congresses in 1775. In September 1775 he was appointed a lieutenant colonel in the 2d North Carolina Continental Regiment. Martin saw military action in South Carolina and won promotion to a colonelcy. He joined Washington's army in 1777, but after the Battle of Germantown he was arrested for cowardice. A court-martial tried and acquitted Martin, but he resigned his commission on November 22, 1777.

Martin's misfortune in the army did not impede his political career. The year after his court-martial he entered the North Carolina Senate, where he served for eight years (1778-82, 1785, and 1787-88). For every session except those of 1778-79, Martin served as speaker. From 1780 to 1781 he also sat on the Board of War and its successor, the Council Extraordinary. In 1781 Martin became acting governor of the state, and in 1782 through 1785 he was elected in his own right.

After his 1785 term in the North Carolina Senate, Martin represented his state in the Continental Congress, but he resigned in 1787. Of the five North Carolina delegates to the Constitutional Convention, Martin was the least strongly Federalist. He did not take an active part in the proceedings, and he left Philadelphia in late August 1787, before the Constitution was signed. Martin was considered a good politician but not suited to public debate. A colleague, Hugh Williamson, remarked that Martin needed time to recuperate after his great exertions as governor "to enable him again to exert his abilities to the advantage of the nation."

Under the new national government, Martin again served as Governor of North Carolina, from 1789 until 1792. After 1790 he moved away from the Federalists to the Republicans. In 1792 Martin, elected by the Republican legislature, entered the U.S. Senate. His vote in favor of the Alien and Sedition Acts cost him reelection. Back in North Carolina, Martin returned to the state senate in 1804 and 1805 to represent Rockingham County. In 1805 he once again served as speaker. From 1790 until 1807 he was a trustee of the University of North Carolina. Martin never married, and he died on November 2, 1807 at the age of 67 at his plantation, "Danbury," in Rockingham County and was buried on the estate.

### Richard Dobbs Spaight, Sr., North Carolina

Spaight was born at New Bern, NC of distinguished English-Irish parentage in 1758. When he was orphaned at eight years of age, his guardians sent him to Ireland, where he obtained an excellent education. He apparently graduated from Scotland's Glasgow University before he returned to North Carolina in 1778.

At that time, the War for Independence was in full swing, and Spaight's superior attainments soon gained him a commission. He became an aide to the state militia commander and in 1780 took part in the Battle of Camden, SC. The year before, he had been elected to the lower house of the legislature.

In 1781 Spaight left the military service to devote full time to his legislative duties. He represented New Bern and Craven County (1781-83 and 1785-87); in 1785 he became speaker. Between terms, he also served in the Continental Congress (1783-85).

In 1787, at the age of 29, Spaight joined the North Carolina delegation to the Philadelphia convention. He was not a leader but spoke on several occasions and numbered among those who attended every session. After the convention, he worked in his home state for acceptance of the Constitution.

Spaight met defeat in bids for the governorship in 1787 and the U.S. Senate two years later. From then until 1792, illness forced his retirement from public life, during which time he visited the West Indies, but he captured the governorship in the latter year (1792-95). In 1793 he served as presidential elector. Two years later, he wed Mary Leach, who bore three children.

In 1798 Spaight entered the U.S. House of Representatives as a Democratic-Republican and remained in office until 1801. During this time, he advocated repeal of the Alien and Sedition Acts and voted for Jefferson in the contested election of 1800. The next year, Spaight was voted into the lower house of the North Carolina legislature; the following year, to the upper.

Only 44 years old in 1802, Spaight was struck down in a duel at New Bern with a political rival, Federalist John Stanly. So ended the promising career of one of the state's foremost leaders. He was buried in the family sepulcher at Clermont estate, near New Bern.

## Hugh Williamson, North Carolina

The versatile Williamson was born of Scotch-Irish descent at West Nottingham, PA., in 1735. He was the eldest son in a large family, whose head was a clothier. Hoping he would become a Presbyterian minister, his parents oriented his education toward that calling. After attending preparatory schools at New London Cross Roads, DE, and Newark, DE, he entered the first class of the College of Philadelphia (later part of the University of Pennsylvania) and took his degree in 1757.

The next two years, at Shippensburg, PA, Williamson spent settling his father's estate. Then training in Connecticut for the ministry, he soon became a licensed Presbyterian preacher but was never ordained. Around this time, he also took a position as professor of mathematics at his alma mater.

In 1764 Williamson abandoned these pursuits and studied medicine at Edinburgh, London, and Utrecht, eventually obtaining a degree from the University of Utrecht. Returning to Philadelphia, he began to practice but found it to be emotionally exhausting. His pursuit of scientific interests continued, and in 1768 he became a member of the American Philosophical Society. The next year, he served on a commission that observed the transits of Venus and Mercury. In 1771 he wrote An Essay on Comets, in which he advanced several original ideas. As a result, the University of Leyden awarded him an LL.D. degree.

In 1773, to raise money for an academy in Newark, DE., Williamson made a trip to the West Indies and then to Europe. Sailing from Boston, he saw the Tea Party and carried news of it to London. When the British Privy Council called on him to testify as to what he had seen, he warned the councilors that the colonies would rebel if the British did not change their policies. While in England, he struck up a close friendship with fellow-scientist Benjamin Franklin, and they cooperated in electrical experiments. Moreover, Williamson furnished to Franklin the letters of Massachusetts Royal Governor Thomas Hutchinson to his lieutenant governor that created a sensation and tended to further alienate the mother country and colonies. In 1775 a pamphlet Williamson had written while in England, called The

Plea of the Colonies, was published. It solicited the support of the English Whigs for the American cause. When the United States proclaimed their independence the next year, Williamson was in the Netherlands. He soon sailed back to the United States, settling first in Charleston, SC, and then in Edenton, NC. There, he prospered in a mercantile business that traded with the French West Indies and once again took up the practice of medicine.

Williamson applied for a medical post with the patriot forces, but found all such positions filled. The governor of North Carolina, however, soon called on his specialized skills, and he became surgeon-general of state troops. After the Battle of Camden, SC, he frequently crossed British lines to tend to the wounded. He also prevented sickness among the troops by paying close attention to food, clothing, shelter, and hygiene.

After the war, Williamson began his political career. In 1782 he was elected to the lower house of the state legislature and to the Continental Congress. Three years later, he left Congress and returned to his legislative seat. In 1786 he was chosen to represent his state at the Annapolis Convention but arrived too late to take part. The next year, he again served in Congress (1787-89) and was chosen as a delegate to the Constitutional Convention. Attending faithfully and demonstrating keen debating skill, he served on five committees, notably on the Committee on Postponed Matters, and played a significant part in the proceedings, particularly the major compromise on representation.

After the convention, Williamson worked for ratification of the Constitution in North Carolina. In 1788 he was chosen to settle outstanding accounts between the state and the federal government. The next year, he was elected to the first U.S. House of Representatives, where he served two terms. In 1789 he married Maria Apthorpe, who bore at least two sons.

In 1793 Williamson moved to New York City to facilitate his literary and philanthropic pursuits. Over the years, he published many political, educational, economic, historical, and scientific works, but the last earned him the most praise. The University of Leyden awarded him an honorary degree. In addition, he was an original trustee of the University of North Carolina and later held trusteeships at the College of Physicians and Surgeons and the University of the State of New York. He was also a founder of the Literary and Philosophical Society of New York and a prominent member of the New-York Historical Society.

In 1819, at the age of 83, Williamson died in New York City and was buried at Trinity Church.

## The Founding Fathers: Pennsylvania

### George Clymer, Pennsylvania

Clymer was orphaned in 1740, only a year after his birth in Philadelphia. A wealthy uncle reared and informally educated him and advanced him from clerk to full-fledged partner in his mercantile firm, which on his death he bequeathed to his ward. Later Clymer merged operations with the Merediths, a prominent business family, and cemented the relationship by marrying his senior partner's daughter, Elizabeth, in 1765.

Motivated at least partly by the impact of British economic restrictions on his business, Clymer early adopted the Revolutionary cause and was one of the first to recommend independence. He attended patriotic meetings, served on the Pennsylvania council of safety, and in 1773 headed a committee that forced the resignation of Philadelphia tea consignees appointed by Britain under the Tea Act. Inevitably, in light of his economic background, he channeled his energies into financial matters. In 1775-76 he acted as one of the first two Continental treasurers, even personally underwriting the war by exchanging all his own specie for Continental currency.

In the Continental Congress (1776-77 and 1780-82) the quiet and unassuming Clymer rarely spoke in debate but made his mark in committee efforts, especially those pertaining to commerce, finance, and military affairs. During the War for Independence, he also served on a series of commissions that conducted important field investigations. In December 1776, when Congress fled from Philadelphia to Baltimore, he and George Walton and Robert Morris remained behind to carry on congressional business. Within a year, after their victory at the Battle of Brandywine, Pa. (September 11, 1777), British troops advancing on Philadelphia detoured for the purpose of vandalizing Clymer's home in Chester County about 25 miles outside the city. His wife and children hid nearby in the woods.

After a brief retirement following his last term in the Continental Congress, Clymer was reelected for the years 1784-88 to the Pennsylvania legislature, where he had also served part time in 1780-82 while still in Congress. As a state legislator, he advocated a bicameral legislature and reform of the penal code and opposed capital punishment. At the Constitutional Convention, where he rarely missed a meeting, he spoke seldom but effectively and played a modest role in shaping the final document.

The next phase of Clymer's career consisted of service in the U.S. House of Representatives in the First Congress (1789-91), followed by appointment as collector of excise taxes on alcoholic beverages in Pennsylvania (1791-94). In 1795-96 he sat on a Presidential commission that negotiated a treaty with the Cherokee and Creek Indians in Georgia. During his retirement, Clymer advanced various community projects, including the Philadelphia Society for Promoting Agriculture and the Pennsylvania Academy of the Fine Arts, and served as the first president of the Philadelphia Bank. At the age of 73, in 1813, he died at Summerseat, an estate a few miles outside Philadelphia at Morrisville that he had purchased and moved to in 1806. His grave is in the Friends Meeting House Cemetery at Trenton, NJ.

## Thomas Fitzsimons, Pennsylvania

Fitzsimons (FitzSimons; Fitzsimmons) was born in Ireland in 1741. Coming to America about 1760, he pursued a mercantile career in Philadelphia. The next year, he married Catherine Meade, the daughter of a prominent local merchant, Robert Meade, and not long afterward went into business with one of his brothers-in-law. The firm of George Meade and Company soon became one of the leading commercial houses in the city and specialized in the West India trade.

When the Revolution erupted, Fitzsimons enthusiastically endorsed the Whig position. During the war, he commanded a company of militia (1776-77). He also sat on the Philadelphia committee of correspondence, council of safety, and navy board. His firm provided supplies and "fire" ships to the military forces and, toward the end of the war, donated £: 5,000 to the Continental Army.

In 1782-83 Fitzsimons entered politics as a delegate to the Continental Congress. In the latter year, he became a member of the Pennsylvania council of censors and served as a legislator (1786-89). His attendance at the Constitutional Convention was regular, but he did not make any outstanding contributions to the proceedings. He was, however, a strong nationalist.
After the convention, Fitzsimons continued to demonstrate his nationalistic proclivities as a three-term U.S. representative (1789-95). He allied himself closely with the program of Hamilton and the emerging Federalist Party. Once again demonstrating his commercial orientation, he advocated a

protective tariff and retirement of the national debt.

Fitzsimons spent most of the remainder of his life in private business, though he retained an interest in public affairs. His views remained essentially Federalist. During the maritime difficulties in the late 1790s, he urged retaliation against British and French interference with American shipping. In the first decade of the 19th century, he vigorously opposed Jefferson's embargo of 1807-9. In 1810, again clashing with the Jeffersonians, he championed the recharter of the First United States Bank.

But Fitzsimons's prominence stemmed from his business leadership. In 1781 he had been one of the founders of the Bank of North America. He also helped organize and held a directorship in the Insurance Company of North America and several times acted as president of the Philadelphia Chamber of Commerce. His financial affairs, like those somewhat earlier of his associate and fellow-signer Robert Morris, took a disastrous turn in 1805. He later regained some of his affluence, but his reputation suffered.

Despite these troubles, Fitzsimons never ceased his philanthropy. He was an outstanding supporter of Philadelphia's St. Augustine's Roman Catholic Church. He also strived to improve public education in the commonwealth and served as trustee of the University of Pennsylvania.

Fitzsimons died at Philadelphia in 1811 after seven decades of life. His tomb is there in the graveyard at St. Mary's Roman Catholic Church, which is in present Independence National Historical Park.

## Benjamin Franklin, Pennsylvania

Franklin was born in 1706 at Boston. He was the tenth son of a soap and candlemaker. He received some formal education but was principally self-taught. After serving an apprenticeship to his father between the ages of 10 and 12, he went to work for his half-brother James, a printer. In 1721 the latter founded the New England Courant, the fourth newspaper in the colonies. Benjamin secretly contributed 14 essays to it, his first published writings.

In 1723, because of dissension with his half-brother, Franklin moved to Philadelphia, where he obtained employment as a printer. He spent only a year there and then sailed to London for two more years. Back in Philadelphia, he rose rapidly in the printing industry. He published The

Pennsylvania Gazette (1730-48), which had been founded by another man in 1728, but his most successful literary venture was the annual Poor Richard 's Almanac (1733-58). It won a popularity in the colonies second only to the Bible, and its fame eventually spread to Europe.

Meantime, in 1730 Franklin had taken a common-law wife, Deborah Read, who was to bear him a son and daughter, and he also apparently had children with another nameless woman out of wedlock. By 1748 he had achieved financial independence and gained recognition for his philanthropy and the stimulus he provided to such civic causes as libraries, educational institutions, and hospitals. Energetic and tireless, he also found time to pursue his interest in science, as well as to enter politics.

Franklin served as clerk (1736-51) and member (1751-64) of the colonial legislature and as deputy postmaster of Philadelphia (1737-53) and deputy postmaster general of the colonies (1753-74). In addition, he represented Pennsylvania at the Albany Congress (1754), called to unite the colonies during the French and Indian War. The congress adopted his "Plan of Union," but the colonial assemblies rejected it because it encroached on their powers.

During the years 1757-62 and 1764-75, Franklin resided in England, originally in the capacity of agent for Pennsylvania and later for Georgia, New Jersey, and Massachusetts. During the latter period, which coincided with the growth of colonial unrest, he underwent a political metamorphosis. Until then a contented Englishman in outlook, primarily concerned with Pennsylvania provincial politics, he distrusted popular movements and saw little purpose to be served in carrying principle to extremes. Until the issue of parliamentary taxation undermined the old alliances, he led the Quaker party attack on the Anglican proprietary party and its Presbyterian frontier allies. His purpose throughout the years at London in fact had been displacement of the Penn family administration by royal authority-the conversion of the province from a proprietary to a royal colony.

It was during the Stamp Act crisis that Franklin evolved from leader of a shattered provincial party's faction to celebrated spokesman at London for American rights. Although as agent for Pennsylvania he opposed by every conceivable means the enactment of the bill in 1765, he did not at first realize the depth of colonial hostility. He regarded passage as unavoidable and preferred to submit to it while actually working for its repeal.

Franklin's nomination of a friend and political ally as stamp distributor for Pennsylvania, coupled with his apparent acceptance of the legislation, armed his proprietary opponents with explosive issues. Their energetic exploitation of them endangered his reputation at home until reliable information was published demonstrating his unabated opposition to the act. For a time, mob resentment threatened his family and new home in Philadelphia until his tradesmen supporters rallied. Subsequently, Franklin's defense of the American position in the House of Commons during the debates over the Stamp Act's repeal restored his prestige at home.

Franklin returned to Philadelphia in May 1775 and immediately became a distinguished member of the Continental Congress. Thirteen months later, he served on the committee that drafted the Declaration of Independence. He subsequently contributed to the government in other important ways, including service as postmaster general, and took over the duties of president of the Pennsylvania constitutional convention.

But, within less than a year and a half after his return, the aged statesman set sail once again for Europe, beginning a career as diplomat that would occupy him for most of the rest of his life. In the years 1776-79, as one of three commissioners, he directed the negotiations that led to treaties of commerce and alliance with France, where the people adulated him, but he and the other commissioners squabbled constantly. While he was sole commissioner to France (1779-85), he and John Jay and John Adams negotiated the Treaty of Paris (1783), which ended the War for Independence.

Back in the United States, in 1785 Franklin became president of the Supreme Executive Council of Pennsylvania. At the Constitutional Convention, though he did not approve of many aspects of the finished document and was hampered by his age and ill-health, he missed few if any sessions, lent his prestige, soothed passions, and compromised disputes.

In his twilight years, working on his Autobiography, Franklin could look back on a fruitful life as the toast of two continents. Energetic nearly to the last, in 1787 he was elected as first president of the Pennsylvania Society for Promoting the Abolition of Slavery-a cause to which he had committed himself as early as the 1730s. His final public act was signing a memorial to Congress recommending dissolution of the slavery system. Shortly thereafter, in 1790 at the age of 84, Franklin passed away in Philadelphia and was laid to rest in Christ Church Burial Ground.

## Jared Ingersoll, Pennsylvania

The son of Jared Ingersoll, Sr., a British colonial official and later prominent Loyalist, Ingersoll was born at New Haven, CT, in 1749. He received an excellent education and graduated from Yale in 1766. He then oversaw the financial affairs of his father, who had relocated from New Haven to Philadelphia. Later, the youth joined him, took up the study of law, and won admittance to the Pennsylvania bar.

In the midst of the Revolutionary fervor, which neither father nor son shared, in 1773, on the advice of the elder Ingersoll, Jared, Jr., sailed to London and studied law at the Middle Temple. Completing his work in 1776, he made a 2-year tour of the Continent, during which time for some reason he shed his Loyalist sympathies.

Returning to Philadelphia and entering the legal profession, Ingersoll attended to the clients of one of the city's leading lawyers and a family friend, Joseph Reed, who was then occupied with the affairs of the Supreme Executive Council of Pennsylvania. In 1781 Ingersoll married Elizabeth Pettit (Petit). The year before, he had entered politics by winning election to the Continental Congress (1780-81).

Although Ingersoll missed no sessions at the Constitutional Convention, had long favored revision of the Articles of Confederation, and as a lawyer was used to debate, he seldom spoke during the proceedings.

Subsequently, Ingersoll held a variety of public positions: member of the Philadelphia common council (1789); attorney general of Pennsylvania (1790-99 and 1811-17); Philadelphia city solicitor (1798-1801); U.S. District Attorney for Pennsylvania (1800-01); and presiding judge of the Philadelphia District Court (1821-22). Meantime, in 1812, he had been the Federalist Vice-Presidential candidate, but failed to win election.

While pursuing his public activities, Ingersoll attained distinction in his legal practice. For many years, he handled the affairs of Stephen Girard, one of the nation's leading businessmen. In 1791 Ingersoll began to practice before the U.S. Supreme Court and took part in some memorable cases. Although in both Chisholm v. Georgia (1792) and Hylton v. United States (1796) he represented the losing side, his arguments helped to clarify difficult constitutional issues. He also represented fellow-signer William Blount, a senator, when he was threatened with impeachment in the late 1790s.

Ingersoll's long career ended in 1822, when he died less than a week after his 73rd birthday. Survived by three children, he was buried in the cemetery of Philadelphia's First Presbyterian Church.

## Thomas Mifflin, Pennsylvania

A member of the fourth generation of a Pennsylvania Quaker family who had emigrated from England, Mifflin was born at Philadelphia in 1744, the son of a rich merchant and local politician. He studied at a Quaker school and then at the College of Philadelphia (later part of the University of Pennsylvania), from which he won a diploma at the age of 16 and whose interests he advanced for the rest of his life.

Mifflin then worked for four years in a Philadelphia countinghouse. In 1764 he visited Europe, and the next year entered the mercantile business in Philadelphia with his brother. In 1767 he wed Sarah Morris. Although he prospered in business, politics enticed him.

In the Pennsylvania legislature (1772-76), Mifflin championed the colonial position against the crown. In 1774 he attended the Continental Congress (1774-76). Meanwhile, he had helped to raise troops and in May 1775 won appointment as a major in the Continental Army, which caused him to be expelled from his Quaker faith. In the summer of 1775 he first became an aide-de-camp to Washington and then Quartermaster General of the Continental Army. Late in 1775 he became a colonel and in May 1776 a brigadier general. Preferring action to administration, after a time he began to perform his quartermaster duties perfunctorily. Nevertheless, he participated directly in the war effort. He took part in the Battles of Long Island, NY, Trenton, NJ, and Princeton, NJ. Furthermore, through his persuasive oratory, he apparently convinced many men not to leave the military service.

In 1777 Mifflin attained the rank of major general but, restive at criticism of his quartermaster activities, he resigned. About the same time, though he later became a friend of Washington, he became involved in the cabal that advanced Gen. Horatio Gates to replace him in command of the Continental Army. In 1777-78 Mifflin sat on the Congressional Board of War. In the latter year, he briefly reentered the military, but continuing attacks on his earlier conduct of the quartermastership soon led him to resign once more.

Mifflin returned immediately to politics. He sat in the state assembly (1778-79) and again in the Continental Congress (1782-84), from December 1783 to the following June as its president. In 1787 he was chosen to take part in the Constitutional Convention. He attended regularly, but made no speeches and did not play a substantial role.

Mifflin continued in the legislature (1785-88 and 1799-1800); succeeded Franklin as president of the Supreme Executive Council (1788-90); chaired the constitutional convention (1789-90); and held the governorship (1790-99), during which time he affiliated himself with the emerging Democratic-Republican Party.

Although wealthy most of his life, Mifflin was a lavish spender. Pressure from his creditors forced him to leave Philadelphia in 1799, and he died at Lancaster the next year, aged 56. The Commonwealth of Pennsylvania paid his burial expenses at the local Trinity Lutheran Church.

## Gouverneur Morris, Pennsylvania

Gouverneur Morris was born at Morrisania estate, in Westchester (present Bronx) County, NY, in 1752. His family was wealthy and enjoyed a long record of public service. His elder half-brother, Lewis, signed the Declaration of Independence.

Gouverneur was educated by private tutors and at a Huguenot school in New Rochelle. In early life, he lost a leg in a carriage accident. He attended King's College (later Columbia College and University) in New York City, graduating in 1768 at the age of 16. Three years later, after reading law in the city, he gained admission to the bar.

When the Revolution loomed on the horizon, Morris became interested in political affairs. Because of his conservatism, however, he at first feared the movement, which he believed would bring mob rule. Furthermore, some of his family and many of his friends were Loyalists. But, beginning in 1775, for some reason he sided with the Whigs. That same year, representing Westchester County, he took a seat in New York's Revolutionary provincial congress (1775-77). In 1776, when he also served in the militia, along with John Jay and Robert R. Livingston he drafted the first constitution of the state. Subsequently he joined its council of safety (1777).

In 1777-78 Morris sat in the legislature and in 1778-79 in the Continental

Congress, where he numbered among the youngest and most brilliant members. During this period, he signed the Articles of Confederation and drafted instructions for Benjamin Franklin, in Paris, as well as those that provided a partial basis for the treaty ending the War for Independence. Morris was also a close friend of Washington and one of his strongest congressional supporters.

Defeated in his bid for reelection to Congress in 1779 because of the opposition of Gov. George Clinton's faction, Morris relocated to Philadelphia and resumed the practice of law. This temporarily removed him from the political scene, but in 1781 he resumed his public career when he became the principal assistant to Robert Morris, Superintendent of Finance for the United States, to whom he was unrelated. Gouverneur held this position for four years.

Morris emerged as one of the leading figures at the Constitutional Convention. His speeches, more frequent than those by anyone else, numbered 173. Although sometimes presented in a light vein, they were usually substantive. A strong advocate of nationalism and aristocratic rule, he served on many committees, including those on postponed matters and style, and stood in the thick of the decision-making process. Above all, it was apparently he who actually drafted the Constitution. Morris subsequently left public life for a time to devote his attention to business. Having purchased the family home from his half-brother, Lewis, he moved back to New York. Afterward, in 1789, Gouverneur joined in a business venture with Robert Morris, and traveled to France, where he witnessed the beginnings of the French Revolution.

Morris was to remain in Europe for about a decade. In 1790-91 he undertook a diplomatic mission to London to try to negotiate some of the outstanding problems between the United States and Great Britain. The mission failed, but in 1792 Washington appointed him as Minister to France, to replace Thomas Jefferson. Morris was recalled two years later but did not come home. Instead, he traveled extensively in Europe for more than four years, during which time he handled his complicated business affairs and contemplated the complex political situation.

Morris returned to the United States in 1799. The next year, he was elected to finish an unexpired term in the U.S. Senate. An ardent Federalist, he was defeated in his bid for reelection in 1802 and left office the following year.

Morris retired to a glittering life at Morrisania, where he had built a new residence. In 1809 he married Anne Cary (Carey) Randolph of Virginia, and they had one son. During his last years, he continued to speak out against the Democratic-Republicans and violently opposed the War of 1812. In the years 1810-13 he served as chairman of the Erie Canal Commission.

Morris died at Morrisania in 1816 at the age of 64 and was buried at St. Anne's Episcopal Churchyard, in the Bronx, New York City.

## Robert Morris, Pennsylvania

Robert Morris was born at or near Liverpool, England, in 1734. When he reached 13 years of age, he emigrated to Maryland to join his father, a tobacco exporter at Oxford, MD. After brief schooling at Philadelphia, the youth obtained employment with Thomas and Charles Willing's well-known shipping-banking firm. In 1754 he became a partner and for almost four decades was one of the company's directors as well as an influential Philadelphia citizen. Wedding Mary White at the age of 35, he fathered five sons and two daughters.

During the Stamp Act turmoil in 1765, Morris joined other merchants in protest, but not until the outbreak of hostilities a decade later did he fully commit himself to the Revolution. In 1775 the Continental Congress contracted with his firm to import arms and ammunition, and he was elected to the Pennsylvania council of safety (1775-76), the committee of correspondence, the provincial assembly (1775-76), the legislature (1776-78), and the Continental Congress (1775-78). In the last body, on July 1, 1776, he voted against independence, which he personally considered premature, but the next day he purposely absented himself to facilitate an affirmative ballot by his delegation.

Morris, a key congressman, specialized in financial affairs and military procurement. Although he and his firm profited handsomely, had it not been for his assiduous labors the Continental Army would probably have been forced to demobilize. He worked closely with General Washington, wheedled money and supplies from the states, borrowed money in the face of overwhelming difficulties, and on occasion even obtained personal loans to further the war cause.

Immediately following his congressional service, Morris sat for two more terms in the Pennsylvania legislature (1778-81). During this time,

Thomas Paine and others attacked him for profiteering in Congress, which investigated his accounts and vindicated him. Nevertheless, his reputation suffered.

Morris embarked on the most dramatic phase of his career by accepting the office of Superintendent of Finance (1781-84) under the Articles of Confederation. Congress, recognizing the perilous state of the nation's finances and its impotence to provide remedies, granted him dictatorial powers and acquiesced to his condition that he be allowed to continue his private commercial enterprises. He slashed all governmental and military expenditures, personally purchased army and navy supplies, tightened accounting procedures, prodded the states to fulfill quotas of money and supplies, and when necessary strained his personal credit by issuing notes over his own signature or borrowing from friends.

To finance Washington's Yorktown campaign in 1781, in addition to the above techniques, Morris obtained a sizable loan from France. He used part of it, along with some of his own fortune, to organize the Bank of North America, chartered that December. The first government-incorporated bank in the United States, it aided war financing.

Although Morris was reelected to the Pennsylvania legislature for 1785-86, his private ventures consumed most of his time. In the latter year, he attended the Annapolis Convention, and the following year the Constitutional Convention, where he sympathized with the Federalists but was, for a man of his eminence, strangely silent. Although in attendance at practically every meeting, he spoke only twice in debates and did not serve on any committees. In 1789, declining Washington's offer of appointment as the first Secretary of the Treasury, he took instead a U.S. Senate seat (1789-95).

During the later years of his public life, Morris speculated wildly, often on overextended credit, in lands in the West and at the site of Washington, DC. To compound his difficulties, in 1794 he began constructing on Philadelphia's Chestnut Street a mansion designed by Maj. Pierre Charles L'Enfant. Not long thereafter, Morris attempted to escape creditors by retreating to The Hills, the country estate along the Schuylkill River on the edge of Philadelphia that he had acquired in 1770.

Arrested at the behest of creditors in 1798 and forced to abandon completion of the mansion, thereafter known in its unfinished state as "Morris' Folly,"

Morris was thrown into the Philadelphia debtor's prison, where he was nevertheless well treated. By the time he was released in 1801, under a federal bankruptcy law, however, his property and fortune had vanished, his health had deteriorated, and his spirit had been broken. He lingered on in poverty and obscurity, living in a simple Philadelphia home on an annuity obtained for his wife by fellow-signer Gouverneur Morris.

Robert Morris died in 1806 in his 73rd year and was buried in the yard of Christ Church.

## James Wilson, Pennsylvania

Wilson was born in 1741 or 1742 at Carskerdo, near St. Andrews, Scotland, and educated at the universities of St. Andrews, Glasgow, and Edinburgh. He then emigrated to America, arriving in the midst of the Stamp Act agitations in 1765. Early the next year, he accepted a position as Latin tutor at the College of Philadelphia (later part of the University of Pennsylvania) but almost immediately abandoned it to study law under John Dickinson.

In 1768, the year after his admission to the Philadelphia bar, Wilson set up practice at Reading, Pa. Two years later, he moved westward to the Scotch-Irish settlement of Carlisle, and the following year he took a bride, Rachel Bird. He specialized in land law and built up a broad clientele. On borrowed capital, he also began to speculate in land. In some way he managed, too, to lecture on English literature at the College of Philadelphia, which had awarded him an honorary master of arts degree in 1766.

Wilson became involved in Revolutionary politics. In 1774 he took over chairmanship of the Carlisle committee of correspondence, attended the first provincial assembly, and completed preparation of Considerations on the Nature and Extent of the Legislative Authority of the British Parliament. This tract circulated widely in England and America and established him as a Whig leader.

The next year, Wilson was elected to both the provincial assembly and the Continental Congress, where he sat mainly on military and Indian affairs committees. In 1776, reflecting the wishes of his constituents, he joined the moderates in Congress voting for a 3-week delay in considering Richard Henry Lee's resolution of June 7th for independence. On the July 1 and 2 ballots on the issue, however, he voted in the affirmative and signed the Declaration of Independence on August 2.

Wilson's strenuous opposition to the republican Pennsylvania constitution of 1776, besides indicating a switch to conservatism on his part, led to his removal from Congress the following year. To avoid the clamor among his frontier constituents, he repaired to Annapolis during the winter of 1777-78 and then took up residence in Philadelphia.

Wilson affirmed his newly assumed political stance by closely identifying with the aristocratic and conservative republican groups, multiplying his business interests, and accelerating his land speculation. He also took a position as Advocate General for France in America (1779-83), dealing with commercial and maritime matters, and legally defended Loyalists and their sympathizers.

In the fall of 1779, during a period of inflation and food shortages, a mob which included many militiamen and was led by radical constitutionalists, set out to attack the republican leadership. Wilson was a prime target. He and some 35 of his colleagues barricaded themselves in his home at Third and Walnut Streets, thereafter known as "Fort Wilson." During a brief skirmish, several people on both sides were killed or wounded. The shock cooled sentiments and pardons were issued all around, though major political battles over the commonwealth constitution still lay ahead.

During 1781 Congress appointed Wilson as one of the directors of the Bank of North America, newly founded by his close associate and legal client Robert Morris. In 1782, by which time the conservatives had regained some of their power, the former was reelected to Congress, and he also served in the period 1785-87.

Wilson reached the apex of his career in the Constitutional Convention (1787), where his influence was probably second only to that of Madison. Rarely missing a session, he sat on the Committee of Detail and in many other ways applied his excellent knowledge of political theory to convention problems. Only Gouverneur Morris delivered more speeches.

That same year, overcoming powerful opposition, Wilson led the drive for ratification in Pennsylvania, the second state to endorse the instrument. The new commonwealth constitution, drafted in 1789-90 along the lines of the U.S. Constitution, was primarily Wilson's work and represented the climax of his 14-year fight against the constitution of 1776.

For his services in the formation of the federal government, though Wilson expected to be appointed Chief Justice of the Supreme Court, in 1789 President Washington named him as an associate justice. He was chosen that same year as the first law professor at the College of Philadelphia. Two years later he began an official digest of the laws of Pennsylvania, a project he never completed, though he carried on for a while after funds ran out.

Wilson, who wrote only a few opinions, did not achieve the success on the Supreme Court that his capabilities and experience promised. Indeed, during those years he was the object of much criticism and barely escaped impeachment. For one thing, he tried to influence the enactment of legislation in Pennsylvania favorable to land speculators. Between 1792 and 1795 he also made huge but unwise land investments in western New York and Pennsylvania, as well as in Georgia. This did not stop him from conceiving a grandiose but ill-fated scheme, involving vast sums of European capital, for the recruitment of European colonists and their settlement in the West. Meantime, in 1793, as a widower with six children, he remarried to Hannah Gray; their one son died in infancy.

Four years later, to avoid arrest for debt, the distraught Wilson moved from Philadelphia to Burlington, NJ. The next year, apparently while on federal circuit court business, he arrived at Edenton, NC, in a state of acute mental stress and was taken into the home of James Iredell, a fellow Supreme Court justice. He died there within a few months. Although first buried at Hayes Plantation near Edenton, his remains were later reinterred in the yard of Christ Church at Philadelphia.

### The Founding Fathers: South Carolina

### Pierce Butler, South Carolina

One of the most aristocratic delegates at the convention, Butler was born in 1744 in County Carlow, Ireland. His father was Sir Richard Butler, member of Parliament and a baronet.

Like so many younger sons of the British aristocracy who could not inherit their fathers' estates because of primogeniture, Butler pursued a military career. He became a major in His Majesty's 29th Regiment and during the colonial unrest was posted to Boston in 1768 to quell disturbances there. In 1771 he married Mary Middleton, daughter of a wealthy South Carolinian, and before long resigned his commission to take up a planter's life in the Charleston area. The couple was to have at least one daughter.

When the Revolution broke out, Butler took up the Whig cause. He was elected to the assembly in 1778, and the next year he served as adjutant general in the South Carolina militia. While in the legislature through most of the 1780s, he took over leadership of the democratic upcountry faction in the state and refused to support his own planter group. The War for Independence cost him much of his property, and his finances were so precarious for a time that he was forced to travel to Amsterdam to seek a personal loan. In 1786 the assembly appointed him to a commission charged with settling a state boundary dispute.

The next year, Butler won election to both the Continental Congress (1787-88) and the Constitutional Convention. In the latter assembly, he was an outspoken nationalist who attended practically every session and was a key spokesman for the Madison-Wilson caucus. Butler also supported the interests of southern slaveholders. He served on the Committee on Postponed Matters.

On his return to South Carolina Butler defended the Constitution but did not participate in the ratifying convention. Service in the U.S. Senate (1789-96) followed. Although nominally a Federalist, he often crossed party lines. He supported Hamilton's fiscal program but opposed Jay's Treaty and Federalist judiciary and tariff measures.

Out of the Senate and back in South Carolina from 1797 to 1802, Butler was considered for but did not attain the governorship. He sat briefly in the Senate again in 1803-4 to fill out an unexpired term, and he once again demonstrated party independence. But, for the most part, his later career was spent as a wealthy planter. In his last years, he moved to Philadelphia, apparently to be near a daughter who had married a local physician. Butler died there in 1822 at the age of 77 and was buried in the yard of Christ Church.

## Charles Pinckney, South Carolina

Charles Pinckney, the second cousin of fellow-signer Charles Cotesworth Pinckney, was born at Charleston, SC, in 1757. His father, Col. Charles Pinckney, was a rich lawyer and planter, who on his death in 1782 was to bequeath Snee Farm, a country estate outside the city, to his son Charles. The latter apparently received all his education in the city of his birth, and he started to practice law there in 1779.

About that time, well after the War for Independence had begun, young Pinckney enlisted in the militia, though his father demonstrated ambivalence about the Revolution. He became a lieutenant, and served at the siege of Savannah (September-October 1779). When Charleston fell to the British the next year, the youth was captured and remained a prisoner until June 1781.

Pinckney had also begun a political career, serving in the Continental Congress (1777-78 and 1784-87) and in the state legislature (1779-80, 1786-89, and 1792-96). A nationalist, he worked hard in Congress to ensure that the United States would receive navigation rights to the Mississippi and to strengthen congressional power.

Pinckney's role in the Constitutional Convention is controversial. Although one of the youngest delegates, he later claimed to have been the most influential one and contended he had submitted a draft that was the basis of the final Constitution. Most historians have rejected this assertion. They do, however, recognize that he ranked among the leaders. He attended full time, spoke often and effectively, and contributed immensely to the final draft and to the resolution of problems that arose during the debates. He also worked for ratification in South Carolina (1788). That same year, he married Mary Eleanor Laurens, daughter of a wealthy and politically powerful South Carolina merchant; she was to bear at least three children.

Subsequently, Pinckney's career blossomed. From 1789 to 1792 he held the governorship of South Carolina, and in 1790 chaired the state constitutional convention. During this period, he became associated with the Federalist Party, in which he and his cousin Charles Cotesworth Pinckney were leaders. But, with the passage of time, the former's views began to change. In 1795 he attacked the Federalist backed Jay's Treaty and increasingly began to cast his lot with Carolina back-country Democratic-Republicans against his own eastern aristocracy. In 1796 he became governor once again, and in 1798 his Democratic-Republican supporters helped him win a seat in the U.S. Senate. There, he bitterly opposed his former party, and in the presidential election of 1800 served as Thomas Jefferson's campaign manager in South Carolina.

The victorious Jefferson appointed Pinckney as Minister to Spain (1801-5), in which capacity he struggled valiantly but unsuccessfully to win cession of the Floridas to the United States and facilitated Spanish acquiescence in the transfer of Louisiana from France to the United States in 1803.

Upon completion of his diplomatic mission, his ideas moving ever closer to democracy, Pinckney headed back to Charleston and to leadership of the state Democratic-Republican Party. He sat in the legislature in 1805-6 and then was again elected as governor (1806-8). In this position, he favored legislative reapportionment, giving better representation to back-country districts, and advocated universal white manhood suffrage. He served again in the legislature from 1810 to 1814 and then temporarily withdrew from politics. In 1818 he won election to the U.S. House of Representatives, where he fought against the Missouri Compromise.

In 1821, Pinckney's health beginning to fail, he retired for the last time from politics. He died in 1824, just three days after his 67th birthday. He was laid to rest in Charleston at St. Philip's Episcopal Churchyard.

## Charles Cotesworth Pinckney, South Carolina

The eldest son of a politically prominent planter and a remarkable mother who introduced and promoted indigo culture in South Carolina, Charles Cotesworth Pinckney was born in 1746 at Charleston. Only seven years later, he accompanied his father, who had been appointed colonial agent for South Carolina, to England. As a result, the youth enjoyed a European education.

Pinckney received tutoring in London, attended several preparatory schools, and went on to Christ Church College, Oxford, where he heard the lectures of the legal authority Sir William Blackstone and graduated in 1764. Pinckney next pursued legal training at London's Middle Temple and was accepted for admission into the English bar in 1769. He then spent part of a year touring Europe and studying chemistry, military science, and botany under leading authorities.

Late in 1769, Pinckney sailed home and the next year entered practice in South Carolina. His political career began in 1769, when he was elected to the provincial assembly. In 1773 he acted as attorney general for several towns in the colony. By 1775 he had identified with the patriot cause and that year sat in the provincial congress. Then, the next year, he was elected to the local committee of safety and made chairman of a committee that drew up a plan for the interim government of South Carolina.

When hostilities broke out, Pinckney, who had been a royal militia officer since 1769, pursued a full-time military calling. When South Carolina organized its forces in 1775, he joined the First South Carolina Regiment as a captain. He soon rose to the rank of colonel and fought in the South in defense of Charleston and in the North at the Battles of Brandywine, PA, and Germantown, PA. He commanded a regiment in the campaign against the British in the Floridas in 1778 and at the siege of Savannah. When Charleston fell in 1780, he was taken prisoner and held until 1782. The following year, he was discharged as a brevet brigadier general.

After the war, Pinckney resumed his legal practice and the management of estates in the Charleston area but found time to continue his public service, which during the war had included tours in the lower house of the state legislature (1778 and 1782) and the senate (1779).

Pinckney was one of the leaders at the Constitutional Convention. Present at all the sessions, he strongly advocated a powerful national government. His proposal that senators should serve without pay was not adopted, but he exerted influence in such matters as the power of the Senate to ratify treaties and the compromise that was reached concerning abolition of the international slave trade. After the convention, he defended the Constitution in South Carolina.

Under the new government, Pinckney became a devoted Federalist. Between 1789 and 1795 he declined presidential offers to command the U.S. Army and to serve on the Supreme Court and as Secretary of War and Secretary of State. In 1796, however, he accepted the post of Minister to France, but the revolutionary regime there refused to receive him and he was forced to proceed to the Netherlands. The next year, though, he returned to France when he was appointed to a special mission to restore relations with that country. During the ensuing XYZ affair, refusing to pay a bribe suggested by a French agent to facilitate negotiations, he was said to have replied "No! No! Not a sixpence!"

When Pinckney arrived back in the United States in 1798, he found the country preparing for war with France. That year, he was appointed as a major general in command of American forces in the South and served in that capacity until 1800, when the threat of war ended. That year, he represented the Federalists as Vice-Presidential candidate, and in 1804 and 1808 as the Presidential nominee. But he met defeat on all three occasions.

For the rest of his life, Pinckney engaged in legal practice, served at times in the legislature, and engaged in philanthropic activities. He was a charter member of the board of trustees of South Carolina College (later the University of South Carolina), first president of the Charleston Bible Society, and chief executive of the Charleston Library Society. He also gained prominence in the Society of the Cincinnati, an organization of former officers of the War for Independence.

During the later period of his life, Pinckney enjoyed his Belmont estate and Charleston high society. He was twice married; first to Sarah Middleton in 1773 and after her death to Mary Stead in 1786. Survived by three daughters, he died in Charleston in 1825 at the age of 79. He was interred there in the cemetery at St. Michael's Episcopal Church.

## John Rutledge, South Carolina

John Rutledge, elder brother of Edward Rutledge, signer of the Declaration of Independence, was born into a large family at or near Charleston, SC, in 1739. He received his early education from his father, an Irish immigrant and physician, and from an Anglican minister and a tutor. After studying law at London's Middle Temple in 1760, he was admitted to English practice. But, almost at once, he sailed back to Charleston to begin a fruitful legal career and to amass a fortune in plantations and slaves. Three years later, he married Elizabeth Grimke, who eventually bore him 10 children, and moved into a townhouse, where he resided most of the remainder of his life.

In 1761 Rutledge became politically active. That year, on behalf of Christ Church Parish, he was elected to the provincial assembly and held his seat until the War for Independence. For 10 months in 1764 he temporarily held the post of provincial attorney general. When the troubles with Great Britain intensified about the time of the Stamp Act in 1765, Rutledge, who hoped to ensure continued self-government for the colonies, sought to avoid severance from the British and maintained a restrained stance. He did, however, chair a committee of the Stamp Act Congress that drew up a petition to the House of Lords.

In 1774 Rutledge was sent to the First Continental Congress, where he pursued a moderate course. After spending the next year in the Second Continental Congress, he returned to South Carolina and helped reorganize its government. In 1776 he served on the committee of safety and took part in the writing of the state constitution. That year, he also became president of the lower house of the legislature, a post he held until 1778. During this period, the new government met many stern tests.

In 1778 the conservative Rutledge, disapproving of democratic revisions in the state constitution, resigned his position. The next year, however, he was elected as governor. It was a difficult time. The British were invading South Carolina, and the military situation was desperate. Early in 1780, by which time the legislature had adjourned, Charleston was besieged. In May it fell, the American army was captured, and the British confiscated Rutledge's property. He ultimately escaped to North Carolina and set about attempting to rally forces to recover South Carolina. In 1781, aided by Gen. Nathanael Greene and a new Continental Army force, he reestablished the government. In January 1782 he resigned the governorship and took a seat in the lower house of the legislature. He never recouped the financial losses he suffered during the war.

In 1782-83 Rutledge was a delegate to the Continental Congress. He next sat on the state chancery court (1784) and again in the lower house of the legislature (1784-90). One of the most influential delegates at the Constitutional Convention, where he maintained a moderate nationalist stance and chaired the Committee of Detail, he attended all the sessions, spoke often and effectively, and served on five committees. Like his fellow South Carolina delegates, he vigorously advocated southern interests.

The new government under the Constitution soon lured Rutledge. He was a Presidential elector in 1789 and Washington then appointed him as Associate Justice of the U.S. Supreme Court, but for some reason he apparently served only a short time. In 1791 he became chief justice of the South Carolina supreme court. Four years later, Washington again appointed him to the U.S. Supreme Court, this time as Chief Justice to replace John Jay. But Rutledge's outspoken opposition to Jay's Treaty (1794), and the intermittent mental illness he had suffered from since the death of his wife in 1792, caused the Federalist-dominated Senate to reject his appointment and end his public career. Meantime, however, he had presided over one term of the Court.

Rutledge died in 1800 at the age of 60 and was interred at St. Michael's Episcopal Church in Charleston.

**The Founding Fathers: Virginia**

**John Blair, Virginia**

A scion of a prominent Virginia family, Blair was born at Williamsburg in

1732. He was the son of John Blair, a colonial official and nephew of James Blair, founder and first president of the College of William and Mary. Signer Blair graduated from that institution and studied law at London's Middle Temple. Thereafter, he practiced at Williamsburg. In the years 1766-70 he sat in the Virginia House of Burgesses as the representative of William and Mary. From 1770 to 1775 he held the position of clerk of the colony's council.

An active patriot, Blair signed the Virginia Association of June 22, 1770, which pledged to abandon importation of British goods until the Townshend Duties were repealed. He also underwrote the Association of May 27, 1774, calling for a meeting of the colonies in a Continental Congress and supporting the Bostonians. He took part in the Virginia constitutional convention (1776), at which he sat on the committee that framed a declaration of rights as well as the plan for a new government. He next served on the Privy Council (1776-78). In the latter year, the legislature elected him as a judge of the General Court, and he soon took over the chief justiceship. In 1780 he won election to Virginia's high chancery court, where his colleague was George Wythe.

Blair attended the Constitutional Convention religiously but never spoke or served on a committee. He usually sided with the position of the Virginia delegation. And, in the commonwealth ratifying convention, Blair helped win backing for the new framework of government.

In 1789 Washington named Blair as an associate justice of the U.S. Supreme Court, where he helped decide many important cases. Resigning that post in 1796, he spent his remaining years in Williamsburg. A widower, his wife (born Jean Balfour) having died in 1792, he lived quietly until he succumbed in 1800. He was 68 years old. His tomb is in the graveyard of Bruton Parish Church.

## James Madison, Virginia

The oldest of 10 children and a scion of the planter aristocracy, Madison was born in 1751 at Port Conway, King George County, VA, while his mother was visiting her parents. In a few weeks she journeyed back with her newborn son to Montpelier estate, in Orange County, which became his lifelong home. He received his early education from his mother, from tutors, and at a private school. An excellent scholar though frail and sickly in his youth, in 1771 he graduated from the College of New Jersey (later

Princeton), where he demonstrated special interest in government and the law. But, considering the ministry for a career, he stayed on for a year of postgraduate study in theology.

Back at Montpelier, still undecided on a profession, Madison soon embraced the patriot cause, and state and local politics absorbed much of his time. In 1775 he served on the Orange County committee of safety; the next year at the Virginia convention, which, besides advocating various Revolutionary steps, framed the Virginia constitution; in 1776-77 in the House of Delegates; and in 1778-80 in the Council of State. His ill health precluded any military service.

In 1780 Madison was chosen to represent Virginia in the Continental Congress (1780-83 and 1786-88). Although originally the youngest delegate, he played a major role in the deliberations of that body. Meantime, in the years 1784-86, he had again sat in the Virginia House of Delegates. He was a guiding force behind the Mount Vernon Conference (1785), attended the Annapolis Convention (1786), and was otherwise highly instrumental in the convening of the Constitutional Convention in 1787. He had also written extensively about deficiencies in the Articles of Confederation.

Madison was clearly the preeminent figure at the convention. Some of the delegates favored an authoritarian central government; others, retention of state sovereignty; and most occupied positions in the middle of the two extremes. Madison, who was rarely absent and whose Virginia Plan was in large part the basis of the Constitution, tirelessly advocated a strong government, though many of his proposals were rejected. Despite his poor speaking capabilities, he took the floor more than 150 times, third only after Gouverneur Morris and James Wilson. Madison was also a member of numerous committees, the most important of which were those on postponed matters and style. His journal of the convention is the best single record of the event. He also played a key part in guiding the Constitution through the Continental Congress.

Playing a lead in the ratification process in Virginia, too, Madison defended the document against such powerful opponents as Patrick Henry, George Mason, and Richard Henry Lee. In New York, where Madison was serving in the Continental Congress, he collaborated with Alexander Hamilton and John Jay in a series of essays that in 1787-88 appeared in the newspapers and were soon published in book form as The Federalist (1788). This set of essays is a classic of political theory and a lucid exposition of the republican principles that dominated the framing of the Constitution.

In the U.S. House of Representatives (1789-97), Madison helped frame and ensure passage of the Bill of Rights. He also assisted in organizing the executive department and creating a system of federal taxation. As leaders of the opposition to Hamilton's policies, he and Jefferson founded the Democratic-Republican Party.

In 1794 Madison married a vivacious widow who was 16 years his junior, Dolley Payne Todd, who had a son; they were to raise no children of their own. Madison spent the period 1797-1801 in semiretirement, but in 1798 he wrote the Virginia Resolutions, which attacked the Alien and Sedition Acts. While he served as Secretary of State (1801-9), his wife often served as President Jefferson's hostess.

In 1809 Madison succeeded Jefferson. Like the first three Presidents, Madison was enmeshed in the ramifications of European wars. Diplomacy had failed to prevent the seizure of U.S. ships, goods, and men on the high seas, and a depression wracked the country. Madison continued to apply diplomatic techniques and economic sanctions, eventually effective to some degree against France. But continued British interference with shipping, as well as other grievances, led to the War of 1812.

The war, for which the young nation was ill prepared, ended in stalemate in December 1814 when the inconclusive Treaty of Ghent which nearly restored prewar conditions, was signed. But, thanks mainly to Andrew Jackson's spectacular victory at the Battle of New Orleans (Chalmette) in January 1815, most Americans believed they had won. Twice tested, independence had survived, and an ebullient nationalism marked Madison's last years in office, during which period the Democratic-Republicans held virtually uncontested sway.

In retirement after his second term, Madison managed Montpelier but continued to be active in public affairs. He devoted long hours to editing his journal of the Constitutional Convention, which the government was to publish four years after his death. He served as co-chairman of the Virginia constitutional convention of 1829-30 and as rector of the University of Virginia during the period 1826-36. Writing newspaper articles defending the administration of Monroe, he also acted as his foreign policy adviser.

Madison spoke out, too, against the emerging sectional controversy that threatened the existence of the Union. Although a slaveholder all his life, he was active during his later years in the American Colonization Society, whose mission was the resettlement of slaves in Africa.

Madison died at the age of 85 in 1836, survived by his wife and stepson.

**George Mason, Virginia**

In 1725, George Mason was born to George and Ann Thomson Mason. When the boy was 10 years old his father died, and young George's upbringing was left in the care of his uncle, John Mercer. The future jurist's education was profoundly shaped by the contents of his uncle's 1500-volume library, one-third of which concerned the law.

Mason established himself as an important figure in his community. As owner of Gunston Hall he was one of the richest planters in Virginia. In 1750 he married Anne Eilbeck, and in 23 years of marriage they had five sons and four daughters. In 1752 he acquired an interest in the Ohio Company, an organization that speculated in western lands. When the crown revoked the company's rights in 1773, Mason, the company's treasurer, wrote his first major state paper, *Extracts from the Virginia Charters, with Some Remarks upon Them.*

During these years Mason also pursued his political interests. He was a justice of the Fairfax County court, and between 1754 and 1779 Mason was a trustee of the city of Alexandria. In 1759 he was elected to the Virginia House of Burgesses. When the Stamp Act of 1765 aroused outrage in the colonies, George Mason wrote an open letter explaining the colonists' position to a committee of London merchants to enlist their support.

In 1774 Mason again was in the forefront of political events when he assisted in drawing up the Fairfax Resolves, a document that outlined the colonists' constitutional grounds for their objections to the Boston Port Act. Virginia's Declaration of Rights, framed by Mason in 1776, was widely copied in other colonies, served as a model for Jefferson in the first part of the Declaration of Independence, and was the basis for the federal Constitution's Bill of Rights.

The years between 1776 and 1780 were filled with great legislative activity. The establishment of a government independent of Great Britain required the abilities of persons such as George Mason. He supported the disestablishment of the church and was active in the organization of military affairs, especially in the West. The influence of his early work, Extracts from the Virginia Charters, is seen in the 1783 peace treaty with Great Britain, which fixed the Anglo-American boundary at the Great Lakes instead of the Ohio River. After independence, Mason drew up the plan for Virginia's cession of its western lands to the United States.

By the early 1780s, however, Mason grew disgusted with the conduct of public affairs and retired. He married his second wife, Sarah Brent, in 1780. In 1785 he attended the Mount Vernon meeting that was a prelude to the Annapolis convention of 1786, but, though appointed, he did not go to Annapolis.

At Philadelphia in 1787 Mason was one of the five most frequent speakers at the Constitutional Convention. He exerted great influence, but during the last two weeks of the convention he decided not to sign the document.

Mason's refusal prompts some surprise, especially since his name is so closely linked with constitutionalism. He explained his reasons at length, citing the absence of a declaration of rights as his primary concern. He then discussed the provisions of the Constitution point by point, beginning with the House of Representatives. The House he criticized as not truly representative of the nation, the Senate as too powerful. He also claimed that the power of the federal judiciary would destroy the state judiciaries, render justice unattainable, and enable the rich to oppress and ruin the poor. These fears led Mason to conclude that the new government was destined to either become a monarchy or fall into the hands of a corrupt, oppressive aristocracy.

Two of Mason's greatest concerns were incorporated into the Constitution. The Bill of Rights answered his primary objection, and the 11th amendment addressed his call for strictures on the judiciary.

Throughout his career Mason was guided by his belief in the rule of reason and in the centrality of the natural rights of man. He approached problems coolly, rationally, and impersonally. In recognition of his accomplishments and dedication to the principles of the Age of Reason, Mason has been called the American manifestation of the Enlightenment. Mason died on October 7, 1792, and was buried on the grounds of Gunston Hall.

## James McClurg, Virginia

James McClurg was born near Hampton, VA, in 1746. He attended the College of William and Mary and graduated in 1762. McClurg then studied medicine at the University of Edinburgh and received his degree in 1770. He pursued postgraduate medical studies in Paris and London and published Experiments upon the Human Bile and Reflections on the Biliary Secretions (1772) in London. His work and writings were well-received and respected by the medical community, and his article was translated into several languages. In 1773 McClurg returned to Virginia and served as a surgeon in the state militia during the Revolution.

Before the end of the war the College of William and Mary appointed McClurg its professor of anatomy and medicine. The same year, 1779, he married Elizabeth Seldon. James McClurg's reputation continued to grow, and he was regarded as one of the most eminent physicians in Virginia. In 1820 and 1821 he was president of the state medical society.

In addition to his medical practice, McClurg pursued politics. In 1782 James Madison advocated McClurg's appointment as secretary of foreign affairs for the United States but was unsuccessful. When Richard Henry Lee and Patrick Henry declined to serve as representatives to the Constitutional Convention in 1787, McClurg was asked to join Virginia's delegation. In Philadelphia McClurg advocated a life tenure for the President and argued for the ability of the federal government to override state laws. Even as some at the convention expressed apprehension of the powers allotted to the presidency, McClurg championed greater independence of the executive from the legislative branch. He left the convention in early August, however, and did not sign the Constitution.

James McClurg's political service did not end with the convention. During George Washington's administration McClurg served on Virginia's executive council. He died in Richmond, VA, on July 9, 1823.

## Edmund Randolph, Virginia

On August 10, 1753, Edmund Randolph was born in Tazewell Hall, Williamsburg, VA. His parents were Ariana Jenings and John Randolph. Edmund attended the College of William and Mary and continued his education by studying the law under his father's tutelage.

When the Revolution broke out, father and son followed different paths. John Randolph, a Loyalist, followed the royal governor, Lord Dunmore, to England, in 1775. Edmund then lived with his uncle Peyton Randolph, a prominent figure in Virginia politics. During the war Edmund served as an aide-de-camp to General Washington and also attended the convention that adopted Virginia's first state constitution in 1776. He was the convention's youngest member at age 23. Randolph married Elizabeth Nicholas in 1776.

Randolph continued to advance in the political world. He became mayor of Williamsburg and Virginia's attorney-general. In 1779 he was elected to the Continental Congress, and in November 1786 Randolph became Governor of Virginia. In 1786 he was a delegate to the Annapolis Convention.

Four days after the opening of the federal convention in Philadelphia, on May 29, 1787, Edmund Randolph presented the Virginia Plan for creating a new government. This plan proposed a strong central government composed of three branches, legislative, executive, and judicial, and enabled the legislative to veto state laws and use force against states that failed to fulfill their duties. After many debates and revisions, including striking the section permitting force against a state, the Virginia Plan became in large part the basis of the Constitution.

Though Randolph introduced the highly centralized Virginia Plan, he fluctuated between the Federalist and Antifederalist points of view. He sat on the Committee of Detail that prepared a draft of the Constitution, but by the time the document was adopted, Randolph declined to sign. He felt it was not sufficiently republican, and he was especially wary of creating a one-man executive. He preferred a three-man council since he regarded "a unity in the Executive" to be the "foetus of monarchy." In a Letter . . . on the Federal Constitution, dated October 10, 1787, Randolph explained at length his objections to the Constitution. The old Articles of Confederation were inadequate, he agreed, but the proposed new plan of union contained too many flaws. Randolph was a strong advocate of the process of amendment. He feared that if the Constitution were submitted for ratification without leaving the states the opportunity to amend it, the document might be rejected and thus close off any hope of another plan of union. However, he hoped that amendments would be permitted and second convention called to incorporate the changes.

By the time of the Virginia convention for ratification, Randolph supported the Constitution and worked to win his state's approval of it. He stated his reason for his switch: "The accession of eight states reduced our deliberations to the single question of Union or no Union."

Under President Washington, Edmund Randolph became Attorney General of the United States. After Thomas Jefferson resigned as Secretary of State, Randolph assumed that post for the years 1794-95. During the Jefferson-Hamilton conflict he tried to remain unaligned. After retiring from politics in 1795, Randolph resumed his law practice and was regarded as a leading figure in the legal community. During his retirement he wrote a history of Virginia. When Aaron Burr went on trial for treason in 1807, Edmund Randolph acted as his senior counsel. In 1813, at age 60 and suffering from paralysis, Randolph died while visiting Nathaniel Burwell at Carter Hall. His body is buried in the graveyard of the nearby chapel.

## George Washington, Virginia

The eldest of six children from his father's second marriage, George Washington was born into the landed gentry in 1732 at Wakefield Plantation, VA. Until reaching 16 years of age, he lived there and at other plantations along the Potomac and Rappahannock Rivers, including the one that later became known as Mount Vernon. His education was rudimentary, probably being obtained from tutors but possibly also from private schools, and he learned surveying. After he lost his father when he was 11 years old, his half-brother Lawrence, who had served in the Royal Navy, acted as his mentor. As a result, the youth acquired an interest in pursuing a naval career, but his mother discouraged him from doing so.

At the age of 16, in 1748, Washington joined a surveying party sent out to the Shenandoah Valley by Lord Fairfax, a land baron. For the next few years, Washington conducted surveys in Virginia and present West Virginia and gained a lifetime interest in the West. In 1751-52 he also accompanied Lawrence on a visit he made to Barbados, West Indies, for health reasons just before his death.

The next year, Washington began his military career when the royal governor appointed him to an adjutantship in the militia, as a major. That same year, as a gubernatorial emissary, accompanied by a guide, he traveled to Fort Le Boeuf, PA, in the Ohio River Valley, and delivered to French authorities an ultimatum to cease fortification and settlement in English territory. During the trip, he tried to better British relations with various Indian tribes.

In 1754, winning the rank of lieutenant colonel and then colonel in the militia, Washington led a force that sought to challenge French control of the Ohio River Valley, but met defeat at Fort Necessity, PA - an event that helped trigger the French and Indian War (1754-63). Late in 1754, irked by the dilution of his rank because of the pending arrival of British regulars, he resigned his commission. That same year, he leased Mount Vernon, which he was to inherit in 1761.

In 1755 Washington reentered military service with the courtesy title of colonel, as an aide to Gen. Edward Braddock, and barely escaped death when the French defeated the general's forces in the Battle of the Monongahela, PA. As a reward for his bravery, Washington rewon his colonelcy and command of the Virginia militia forces, charged with defending the colony's frontier. Because of the shortage of men and equipment, he found the assignment challenging. Late in 1758 or early in 1759, disillusioned over governmental neglect of the militia and irritated at not rising in rank, he resigned and headed back to Mount Vernon.

Washington then wed Martha Dandridge Custis, a wealthy widow and mother of two children. The marriage produced no offspring, but Washington reared those of his wife as his own. During the period 1759-74, he managed his plantations and sat in the Virginia House of Burgesses. He supported the initial protests against British policies; took an active part in the nonimportation movement in Virginia; and, in time, particularly because of his military experience, became a Whig leader.

By the 1770s, relations of the colony with the mother country had become strained. Measured in his behavior but strongly sympathetic to the Whig position and resentful of British restrictions and commercial exploitation, Washington represented Virginia at the First and Second Continental Congresses. In 1775, after the bloodshed at Lexington and Concord, Congress appointed him as commander in chief of the Continental Army. Overcoming severe obstacles, especially in supply, he eventually fashioned a well-trained and disciplined fighting force.

The strategy Washington evolved consisted of continual harassment of British forces while avoiding general actions. Although his troops yielded much ground and lost a number of battles, they persevered even during the dark winters at Valley Forge, PA, and Morristown, NJ. Finally, with the aid of the French fleet and army, he won a climactic victory at the Battle of Yorktown, VA, in 1781.

During the next two years, while still commanding the agitated Continental Army, which was underpaid and poorly supplied, Washington denounced proposals that the military take over the government, including one that planned to appoint him as king, but supported army petitions to the Continental Congress for proper compensation. Once the Treaty of Paris (1783) was signed, he resigned his commission and returned once again to Mount Vernon. His wartime financial sacrifices and long absence, as well as generous loans to friends, had severely impaired his extensive fortune, which consisted mainly of his plantations, slaves, and landholdings in the West. At this point, however, he was to have little time to repair his finances, for his retirement was brief.

Dissatisfied with national progress under the Articles of Confederation, Washington advocated a stronger central government. He hosted the Mount Vernon Conference (1785) at his estate after its initial meetings in Alexandria, though he apparently did not directly participate in the discussions. Despite his sympathy with the goals of the Annapolis Convention (1786), he did not attend. But, the following year, encouraged by many of his friends, he presided over the Constitutional Convention, whose success was immeasurably influenced by his presence and dignity. Following ratification of the new instrument of government in 1788, the electoral college unanimously chose him as the first President.

The next year, after a triumphal journey from Mount Vernon to New York City, Washington took the oath of office at Federal Hall. During his two precedent-setting terms, he governed with dignity as well as restraint. He also provided the stability and authority the emergent nation so sorely needed, gave substance to the Constitution, and reconciled competing factions and divergent policies within the government and his administration. Although not averse to exercising presidential power, he respected the role of Congress and did not infringe upon its prerogatives. He also tried to maintain harmony between his Secretary of State Thomas Jefferson and Secretary of the Treasury Alexander Hamilton, whose differences typified evolving party divisions from which Washington kept aloof.

Yet, usually leaning upon Hamilton for advice, Washington supported his plan for the assumption of state debts, concurred in the constitutionality of the bill establishing the Bank of the United States, and favored enactment of tariffs by Congress to provide federal revenue and protect domestic manufacturers.

Washington took various other steps to strengthen governmental authority, including suppression of the Whisky Rebellion (1794). To unify the country, he toured the Northeast in 1789 and the South in 1791. During his tenure, the government moved from New York to Philadelphia in 1790, he superintended planning for relocation to the District of Columbia, and he laid the cornerstone of the Capitol (1793).

In foreign affairs, despite opposition from the Senate, Washington exerted dominance. He fostered United States interests on the North American continent by treaties with Britain and Spain. Yet, until the nation was stronger, he insisted on the maintenance of neutrality. For example, when the French Revolution created war between France and Britain, he ignored the remonstrances of pro-French Jefferson and pro-English Hamilton.

Although many people encouraged Washington to seek a third term, he was weary of politics and refused to do so. In his "Farewell Address" (1796), he urged his countrymen to forswear party spirit and sectional differences and to avoid entanglement in the wars and domestic policies of other nations.

Washington enjoyed only a few years of retirement at Mount Vernon. Even then, demonstrating his continued willingness to make sacrifices for his country in 1798 when the nation was on the verge of war with France he agreed to command the army, though his services were not ultimately required. He died at the age of 67 in 1799. In his will, he emancipated his slaves.

## George Wythe, Virginia

George Wythe, the second of Thomas and Margaret Wythe's three children, was born in 1726 on his family's plantation on the Back River in Elizabeth City County, VA. Both parents died when Wythe was young, and he grew up under the guardianship of his older brother, Thomas. Though Wythe was to become an eminent jurist and teacher, he received very little formal education. He learned Latin and Greek from his well-educated mother, and he probably attended for a time a grammar school operated by the College of William and Mary.

Wythe's brother later sent him to Prince George County to read law under an uncle. In 1746, at age 20, he joined the bar, moved to Spotsylvania County, and became associated with a lawyer there. In 1747 he married his partner's sister, Ann Lewis, but she died the next year. In 1754 Lt. Gov. Robert Dinwiddie appointed him as acting colonial attorney general, a position that he held for only a few months. The next year, Wythe's brother died and he inherited the family estate. He chose, however, to live in Williamsburg in the house that his new father-in-law, an architect, designed and built for him and his wife, Elizabeth Taliaferro. They married in 1755, and their only child died in infancy.

At Williamsburg, Wythe immersed himself in further study of the classics and the law and achieved accreditation by the colonial supreme court. He served in the House of Burgesses from the mid-1750s until 1775, first as delegate and after 1769 as clerk. In 1768 he became mayor of Williamsburg, and the next year he sat on the board of visitors of the College of William and Mary. During these years he also directed the legal studies of young scholars, notably Thomas Jefferson. Wythe and Jefferson maintained a lifelong friendship, first as mentor and pupil and later as political allies.

Wythe first exhibited revolutionary leanings in 1764 when Parliament hinted to the colonies that it might impose a stamp tax. By then an experienced legislator, he drafted for the House of Burgesses a remonstrance to Parliament so strident that his fellow delegates modified it before adoption. Wythe was one of the first to express the concept of separate nationhood for the colonies within the British empire.

When war broke out, Wythe volunteered for the army but was sent to the Continental Congress. Although present from 1775 through 1776, Wythe exerted little influence and signed the Declaration of Independence after the formal signing in August 1776. That same year, Wythe, Jefferson, and Edmund Pendleton undertook a three-year project to revise Virginia's legal code. In 1777 Wythe also presided as speaker of the Virginia House of Delegates.

An appointment as one of the three judges of the newly created Virginia high court of chancery followed in 1778. For 28 years, during 13 of which he was the only chancellor, Wythe charted the course of Virginia jurisprudence. In addition, he was an ex officio member of the state superior court.

Wythe's real love was teaching. In 1779 Jefferson and other officials of the College of William and Mary created the first chair of law in a U.S. institution of higher learning and appointed Wythe to fill it. In that position, he educated America's earliest college-trained lawyers, among them John Marshall and James Monroe. In 1787 he attended the Constitutional Convention but played an insignificant role. He left the proceedings early and did not sign the Constitution. The following year, however, he was one of the Federalist leaders at the Virginia ratifying convention. There he presided over the Committee of the Whole and offered the resolution for ratification.

In 1791, the year after Wythe resigned his professorship, his chancery duties caused him to move to Richmond, the state capital. He was reluctant to give up his teaching, however, and opened a private law school. One of his last and most promising pupils was young Henry Clay.

In 1806, in his eightieth year, Wythe died at Richmond under mysterious circumstances, probably of poison administered by his grandnephew and heir, George Wythe Sweeney. Reflecting a lifelong aversion to slavery, Wythe emancipated his slaves in his will. His grave is in the yard of St. John's Episcopal Church in Richmond.

CPSIA information can be obtained
at www.ICGtesting.com
Printed in the USA
BVHW031521020919
557307BV00011B/52/P